THIS WILL BE THE PLACE

Cassina

This Will Be The Place

Thoughts and photographs about the future of interiors

Edited by Felix Burrichter

RIZZOLI
NEW YORK

New York · Paris · London · Milan

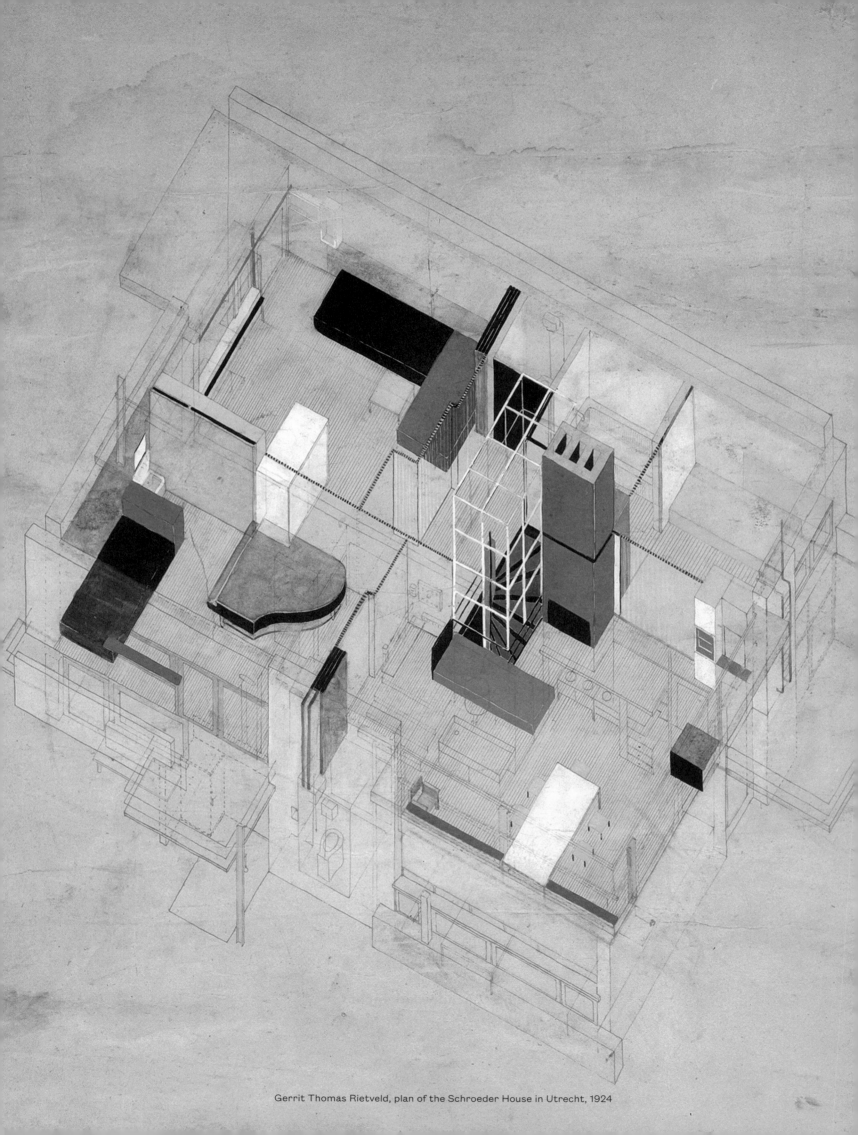

Gerrit Thomas Rietveld, plan of the Schroeder House in Utrecht, 1924

CONTENTS

Beyond the Book of Interiors

A Reflection on Past, Present, and Future.
A Conversation Between Objects for the Home and Interiors

Barbara Lehmann

"The best way to predict the future is to invent it"—Alan Kay

Reflection over the temporal horizons of the past, present, and future is for some a natural inclination. In the ninety years since it was founded, Cassina has consolidated its founders' instincts to join the near past with the future, orienting the company's trajectory between a possible future that is born out of an analysis of sociocultural trends, and an ideal future as a horizon that is continuously being redefined and planned.

Cassina has always supplied the market with furniture and objects that respond to the present: informing the everyday and at the same time feeding the imagination to conjure up new scenarios. The company's cultural contribution to the world of design and interior architecture has constantly been expressed through models conceived not merely as industrial products, but as the expressions of a lifestyle and as tools used to seek new ways of living. This is because those who create culture are asked to shed light, to define the contours of things, to imagine new directions and perspectives.

Tomorrow walks down today's path: this is a concept that was tested from the very beginning by Cesare Cassina, and materialized through excellent collaborations. One such collaboration was with Gio Ponti, for example, whose aim was to introduce a potential narrative of industrialization, of modernism, and of the "Italian home." The sleek, lightweight lines of the products that Ponti created signified a new modernity. The air of the future could be breathed in the interiors of the cruise ships designed by the architect together with Cassina.

These projects were the authentic expression of the excellence of Italian taste, culture, arts, and crafts. They were new products, but also new domestic and collective visions instantly promoted via the company's regular participation in the Triennale and the furniture shows. Whether it was dealing with a "unité d'habitation," a "vacation home," or the choice of "colors and forms in today's home," to mention only the most important exhibitions in the 1950s, Cassina was always at the forefront in the quest to assimilate the modernity in Italian style.

Even the introduction to the Cassina catalogue in the 1960s by such a modern master as Le Corbusier, which may have seemed like an effort to bring back something from the past, was actually an instrument that could be used to look ahead: choosing with conviction the direction of a product line of absolute modernity, aware of the importance of history as a point of reference of excellence and a dialectical pole. There can be no future without a knowledge of the past, especially as concerns the recent and founding past of contemporary aesthetics comprising exemplary models and visionary architectural decor.

Ocean liner *Andrea Doria* ballroom, interiors designed by Cassina with Gio Ponti, 1952

Cab chair by Mario Bellini, Cassina, 1977

La Basilica table by Mario Bellini, Cassina, 1977

CASSINA. THIS WILL BE THE PLACE

The living room of architect Franco Albini's apartment in Milan with the *Veliero* bookcase he designed, 1940

In order to teach people to be aware of the forms that surrounded them, it was important to divulge the principles of modernity and the new interiors that, thanks to a *plan libre*, finally allowed for different types of use: the catalogue was thus enriched with the "domestic equipment" theorized by Le Corbusier, such as the standard *casiers*, which entailed using variously arranged modular elements to articulate spaces. Later, the catalogues would include Rietveld's sculptures, both real and abstract, which created open spatial systems arranged by juxtapositions, where color was an instrument that could be used to determine the relationship between the parts. And then there were the everyday objects *à réaction poétique*, which offered space a meaning, and objects like Albini's poetic tensile structure known as the *Veliero*, an ethereal domestic architecture, a diaphragm suggesting atmospheric spaces.

In shaping new lifestyles, Cassina orchestrated these re-editions of exemplary objects so they would have the chance to convey to everyday life the symbolic value of milestones together with the most avant-garde research that experimented with new materials or a new expressiveness. The aim has always been the search for tangible quality and the content of the single object and of the whole, beyond fleeting fads: it is a collection that is built around different objects, belonging to different personalities.

First of all, it is a solid collection of models that is constantly confronted by a clear desire for classicism. In this regard, the headline of a 1960s advertising campaign, used for the purposes of both contemporary production and the modern masters, read: "Rational structures, classics from the instant they're conceived" [press campaign 1969], a very evident, exemplary statement for a long-lived collection, in perfect harmony with Cassina's philosophy. This was accompanied by a good dose of open-mindedness and transgression so as to foster "a whole new way of living" [press campaign 1971], which reflects an uncommon level of culture and taste, a conception of life that combines prestige with design excellence.

Finally the affirmation, especially in this past decade, of Cassina's multicultural nature thanks to its diversified visions, cross-pollinated with art, fashion, and research, even when the latter is not directly related to furniture, in order to understand the complex world of interior design. To list the most recent ones: artistic collaborations such as the one with Bertjan Pot to create a very fine fabric, a bespoke outfit of sorts, designed to interpret one of the icons of the catalogue; Rietveld's *Utrecht* chair; the implementation of models/works of art like Ron Gilad's mirrors; or the objects in Dino Gavina's *Ultramobile Simon* collection, bringing poetry to the domestic sphere; and, lastly, the more recent connections with the concept of the installation, and the use of contemporary materials—"poor" ones at times—played out in a new dimension in the interiors proposed by art director Patricia Urquiola. Alongside these are important operations aimed at culturally divulging the values of architectural decor, supported by reconstructions not just of furnishings but of entire settings—Le Corbusier's Cabanon, or the futuristic Refuge Tonneau designed in 1939 by Charlotte Perriand and Pierre Jeanneret, portable architecture for extreme environments, the striking forerunners of projects realized many decades later, like the Antarctic research stations. Because here the research is ongoing, from the design stage to the communication phase with dense installations of content.

It is a path that was undertaken in previous decades with visions for the domestic environment that often went beyond what had so far been realized,

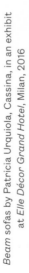

Beam sofas by Patricia Urquiola, Cassina, in an exhibit at Elle Décor Grand Hotel, Milan, 2016

CASSINA. THIS WILL BE THE PLACE

Model of Charlotte Perriand and Pierre Jeanneret's Refuge Tonneau, 1938

Cassina showroom installation inspired by the project
for the Refuge Tonneau, Paris, 2014

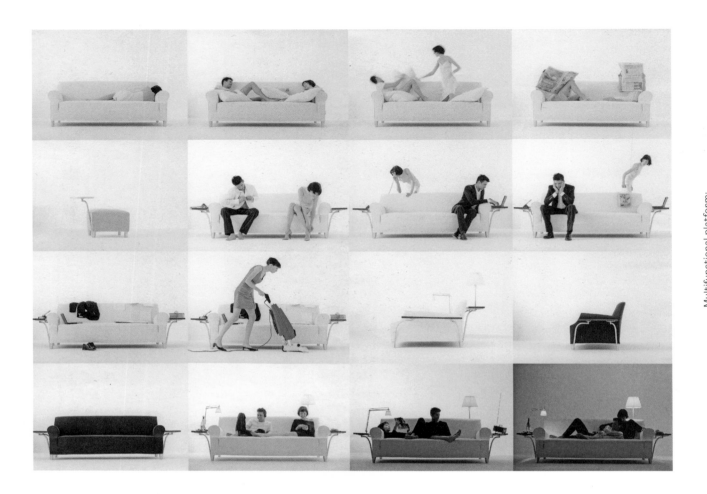

Multifunctional platform:
Philippe Starck's L.W.S. Lazy Working Sofa, Cassina, 1998

Interior with *Piero Lissoni's 8 sofa, Cassina, 2014*

CASSINA. THIS WILL BE THE PLACE

The death of the standard: *Sit Down* armchair designed by Gaetano Pesce, Cassina. Poster made on the occasion of the 1975 Salone del Mobile

such as Philippe Starck's wired multifunctional islands suited to all rhythms of life, or interpretations of contemporaneity like the "quiet" modular upholstered furniture by Piero Lissoni, a prestigious context where icons can fully be appreciated.

An incredible path unfolded, especially in the 1970s, when the search for new models of living was expressed boldly. There was Gaetano Pesce's vision, which promoted the production of a diversified series, against the fundamental idea of the standard and the homologation of our furniture and our interiors; there was the anti-conformist tale of the infinite possibilities of use for the *AEO* model [*Where can I put my* AEO?], the expression of a new freedom achieved and hoped for in that climate of protest—the year was 1968—freedom that could be adapted to the lives of two people, to that of the group, to the context thanks to the different configurations and quick changes in appearance; there were the editions of Bracciodiferro, highly philosophical models, works of art in a limited edition for intellectually elite interiors; and, lastly, there was Mario Bellini's *Kar-a-sutra* car, whose habitat, consisting of a series of plastic pillows that preserved the shape of the user's body, and could easily be used for sleeping, talking, reading, and playing, introduced the idea of the identification between the home and a car suited to a nomadic lifestyle.

The latter project was presented at the famous exhibition *Italy: The New Domestic Landscape*, held in 1972 at the MoMA in New York; it was an apex and also a profound reflection on Italian design. Cassina's participation in that show

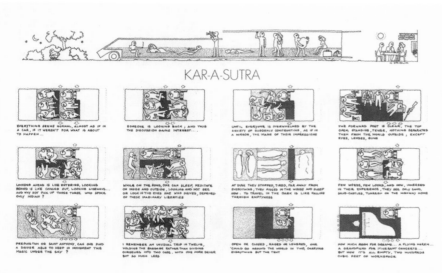

Top: prototype for the *Kar-a-sutra*, a concept car designed by Mario Bellini with Dario Bellini, Francesco Binfaré, Gianfranco Origlia; technical coordination by the Centro Ricerche Cassina, sponsored by Cassina Centro Cassina, C&B Italia Citroën, Industrie Pirelli, 1972
Bottom: Gianfranco Origlia, Drawings for all the possible uses of the *Kar-a-sutra*'s interiors, 1972

was important to understand the trends underway at the time, from the evident tendency to find shelter in a utopian atmosphere, to the need to restore a line of design rationalization. Cassina responded to this dualism in 1977, together with Mario Bellini, by creating a book/catalogue with a very significant title: *Il libro dell'arredamento* (The Furniture Book). An abacus, a taxonomy of interior decor to meet demands for the differentiation of products based on "circumstances of use" and "semantic characteristics"; a reference book for current—or perhaps we should say timeless—models such as the *Cab* chair or the *La Rotonda* table, and its formulation as a complete and organized system with solutions for specific needs. A book/catalogue that, like an encyclopedia, organized each piece of furniture in relation to function and material, suggested how to really decorate a home beyond unlikely, hypothetical scenarios, and thus became a natural starting point for anyone wanting to know more about current trends. That, too, was released on the occasion of an important anniversary for Cassina, its fiftieth.

What is the current "domestic landscape" for Cassina? What will be the place, the home we inhabit? Cassina's answer is *This Will Be the Place*, asking the kaleidoscopic director of an innovative platform for multidisciplinary creatives to draw a map so that we can envision our present lifestyle and that of the near future. Felix Burrichter has thus coordinated with Cassina different contributions by architects, designers, and critics who analyze new social behaviors. Technological acceleration and globalization undoubtedly influence our lives, but what changes have they truly brought about? These readings are summed up in the iconography, translated into visions of interiors that reveal the versatility of the Cassina collection in contexts that feature variable contents, with finespun filters between public and private, spaces steeped in memory or balanced between the natural and the artificial.

It is an ever-changing collection for scenarios that are never conventional, that simultaneously proposes new models with up-to-date formal and semantic codes while also applying evolutionary dynamics to iconic pieces according to a work-in-progress rationale for "unusual conversations."

Advertising poster for the *Golgotha* series by Gaetano Pesce, Bracciodiferro Cassina, 1972

"The LITTLE HOUSEHOLD MONUMENT affords a view from on high, and is a rather unusual position for observation and reconnaissance. It serves as a small monument for home and street; perched on it a normal man may for once be transformed into a personage and expand his personality, exhibit himself, and make speeches to his family or fellow citizens."
—Alessandro Mendini

Alessandro Mendini, *Monumentino da casa*, Bracciodiferro Cassina, 1973

PART I

Four Interviews and One Essay

Introduction

Felix Burrichter

"The future is now!" That old adage... Popular culture, and by extension humankind, is programmed to obsess over not just the now but also the what-comes-after-now, in a never-ending race to stay one step ahead of the game. But while the present is hard enough to grasp (for by the time we think we've nailed it, it's already too late), anticipating the future seems forever doomed to fail. From optimistic predictions of individual space travel to darkly dystopian fantasy landscapes, most of what science-fiction writers and self-proclaimed futurologists imagined for the early twenty-first century has turned out to be wrong. Even fifty years ago few foresaw the rise of the virtual and the digital, which have vastly transformed our daily lives in recent decades. But has the computer revolution affected our living spaces to the same extent it has transformed our working environments? Or have the dwellings we build for comfort, reclusion, or entertainment proven a firewall that still protects us from virtual overreach? For despite all the advances of the digital age, we still cannot eat at virtual dinner tables, lounge on virtual sofas, or sleep in virtual beds. And besides information technology, what else will inflect the evolution of our ideas of domestic bliss as the twenty-first century marches on?

That is why for this book we asked the deceptively naive question: what will the home of the future look like? Or rather, what *could* it look like? What could it *feel* like? For to those who object that predicting the future is a futile exercise, we counter that yesterday's dreams of tomorrow have long nurtured today's attempts to build the present. To help us answer our questions, we asked a group of five experts who all have their own very different theories about the matter. The architectural historian and Princeton scholar Beatriz

Scene from *Sleeper*, directed by Woody Allen, 1973

Scene from *Metropolis* by Fritz Lang, 1927

Scene from *The Matrix*,
directed by Lilly and Lana Wachowski, 1999

INTRODUCTION

23

Colomina (page 36), for example, states that the modern human's identity has for the most part been reduced to the content of his or her smartphone, a device via which almost all social and professional interaction can be carried out. As a result, she says, the twenty-first century will be that of the bed: thanks to laptops, tablet computers, and smartphones, we can all run our entire lives from between the sheets—public and private, work and play, and sleeping and waking all become concentrated in one spot. A similar blurring of boundaries, between public and private, inside and out, is at the core of what Berlin-based architect Arno Brandlhuber (page 48) describes as the future's need for deregulation. Changing demographics require more fluidity in home planning, where the walls between preconceived spatial and societal configurations must be broken down, both literally and figuratively. For Brandlhuber, the answer to life's increasing complexities is more of less.

In his speculative essay "How we Live Tomorrow" (page 68), the Finnish architect and musician Martti Kalliala pushes such ideas to sardonic extremes, imagining domestic scenarios where remote-controlled robots reign supreme over spotlessly antiseptic and empty show homes, or where aggressively agile centenarians maintain their physical prowess thanks to age-appropriate play-dens.

Yet every significant transformation engenders a backlash. In the case of today's hyper-accelerated urbanization and the total permeation of digital technology, the rebound will take the form of a return to nature and to the simplicity of traditional ways of life. At least that's what Chinese architect Zhao Yang predicts (page 58). Hailing from the country that has arguably undergone the most forceful and spectacular transformation of the past thirty years, Yang contends that only by respecting tradition and a sense of place can we ensure ourselves a viable future.

But what all our experts have in common is their belief that, in order to

Scene from 2001–A Space Odyssey by Stanley Kubrick, 1968

Scene from an episode of *The Jetsons*, cartoon series produced by Hanna-Barbera (1962–1963)

Scene of an interior in *Things to Come*, directed by William Cameron Menzies, 1936, installations designed by László Moholy-Nagy

think about the future, one must have a keen understanding of the past and a sharp perception of the present. It's a view that is adroitly summed up by our fifth expert, design icon Konstantin Grcic (page 26), who contends that even what "we consider visionary [with respect to past design], would have been deeply entrenched in the reality of its time. [...] Looking into the future requires confronting reality." Which is precisely what this book sets out to do, embracing the past, assessing the present, while keeping a firm eye on all aspects of the future—the awesome, the awful, and the boldly beautiful.

The future is indeed now. We just have to get ready to face it.

KONSTANTIN GRCIC

Few figures have had a greater impact on the course of industrial design over the past quarter century than Konstantin Grcic. The son of an artist, he initially trained as a cabinetmaker, a hands-on apprenticeship that informed his ability to produce some of the most iconic designs of recent years. Combining an analytical approach, a deep knowledge of art and design history, and a keen interest in technological innovation, Grcic constantly pushes the boundaries of industrial design. While many consider him a visionary, Grcic rejects this title. In order to see the future, he explains, "we must first carefully assess the present."

FELIX BURRICHTER   There's a great quote of yours that's mentioned in the exhibition catalogue for *Panorama*: [*Konstantin Grcic—Panorama*, Vitra Design Museum, Weil am Rhein, 2014] "Good design is not intended to please. It should activate and engage the user and question its own functionality." Could you elaborate a little what you mean by that?

KONSTANTIN GRCIC   The quote expresses my belief that radical design thinking can prevail over the pressure "to please." It must confront a critical discourse instead of making early tradeoffs. That's why working on the *Panorama* exhibition required me to recognize the fundamental issues of my practice. It was an opportunity for me to take stock—but also to look ahead. I deliberately chose the topic of "future" to challenge myself. Unfortunately, the reality of working in a commercial environment has a strong "please the market" element. Challenging the existing norms and projecting ideas beyond staked out territory often gets compromised during the process. Having said that, it was not at all easy to let imagination run wild. I realized that a lack of reality gave rise to speculation, which, in turn, became quite unsustainable.

FB   Because you felt that you'd reached your limits?

KG   Yes. I was missing that handrail of realness, which is actually quite important. Design will never be as detached as art. Design is always earthed in some form of context, a circumstance of conditions that informs a project. Most of the time I regard those conditions as positive and inspirational. And in the attempt to look speculatively into the future it terrified me how much these elements were missing. Good design is extremely precise. It embraces reality, rather than distancing itself from it. This is also true of the past. Historical design that, today, we consider visionary, would have been deeply entrenched in the reality of its time. In other words, looking to the future doesn't start from a blank sheet of paper; in order to see the future we must first assess what there is right in front of us. Seeking out evidence of possible disruptions is where an opportunity for change is likely to be found. Looking into the future requires confronting reality. The aspiration is no longer to create the one big utopia. Real change now tends to play out in smaller steps; it is no longer a "global" plan, but rather one that starts off local. Naturally, we have a much better understanding of what we know firsthand. Even the most future oriented thinking comes from a firm and precise knowledge of a local reality. That's perhaps the essence of my realization. And indeed, most of my work is pretty local—based out of Germany, I am mainly working for European clients. This means that I work with people I know, people I can discuss things with face to face. A factory is a place I can feel and smell. I get to know the workers, see what they do, how they do it. Today, that's a form of dealing with "future" that is more meaningful than making speculations. The world revolves around the very simple, honest, and tangible things, precisely because it's becoming so complex.

FB   Sometimes I get the feeling that the future is already all around us, especially when it comes to design, technology, and materials. That we're always playing catch-up with the future. That we ourselves aren't yet as far along as the possibilities that surround us.

KG   Yes. The problem is that when we think of the future, we picture a certain cliché of it and that is often connected to technology, i.e. electronic, digital, and so on. In contrast to that I work in an industry that's much more analog—namely, furniture. Mine is a slow world, a world in which one scrutinizes and revises the things that have existed for hundreds of years. In that sense, we are not really part of the fu-

ture. On the surface it appears that furniture hasn't really changed that much while our lives have become mobile, networked, independent, emancipated, peripatetic, and so on [Laughs]. The typology of the chair has been around since ancient Egypt, if not longer. But for all its simplicity, it has always had an enormous capacity to adapt or even anticipate the changes in society. I find that incredibly exciting. Examples from my own work that fit this argument are *Chair_ONE* [Magis, 2004] and the *360°* stool [Magis, 2009], *Landen* [Vitra Edition, 2007], or the *Chaos* chair [ClassiCon, 2001]. These are all designs that emerged from a serious examination of the way we sit given that our lives have changed. People might say, "Why another chair?" I still believe that designing furniture can have a big relevance, because it works as a seismograph of our culture and society.

FB   Speaking of *Chair_ONE*: how do you explain its success?

KG   All I can say is that when we made it, it felt like a propulsion. We pushed open some kind of door, and there was something there that dragged us further and further. The entire development has taken four years. And during that whole period, Magis (the client) and we never

Konstantin Grcic, *Kanu* armchair, Cassina, 2008

CASSINA. THIS WILL BE THE PLACE

View of the *Public Space* installation at the *Konstantin Grcic. Panorama* exhibition, Vitra Design Museum, Weil am Rhein and Z33, Hasselt, 2014-2015

felt the need to compromise. It was our project and we were determined to take it all the way. We thought, "Even if nobody else follows, this project is still important for us." When the chair finally came out on market, it attracted a lot of attention, but nobody dared buying it! Not because they didn´t like it, but because it somehow vexed people. The hard material, the latticework... I guess it didn't seem like a chair [Laughs]. But what is a chair anyway? And what makes a good chair? I strongly believe that the adequacy of any chair relates to where it is used, and by whom, and how. I designed *Chair_ONE* to be used in an urban context, i.e. in public spaces, out in the streets. This kind of environment is much more raw than indoors. And it makes you sit in a different way, which means that we are talking about a whole different notion of comfort than what would apply to a domestic chair.

FB   And then there are chairs like *Teepee* and *Kanu*, which you designed in 2008 for Cassina and with which very few people are familiar. These are very, very different from *Chair_ONE*, both in material and design.

KG   True. But they're no less interesting.

That's also why I like to design chairs: each one can be so different. Designing chairs never ceases to be challenging. With every chair we may ask similar questions, but the answers are always new. Of course a chair is a fascinating thing because you come into such direct physical contact with it. Just think of the many ways we sit in chairs. There is no one fixed position, but a multitude of different postures. A good chair becomes part of you, it dresses you. There's a famous test where people rate chairs for comfort, once blindfolded, once not. Their verdicts turn out contradictory. Blindfolded, they experience only the physical comfort of the chair. But when they actually *see* the chair, they let themselves get seduced by its looks. A chair that you find beautiful appears to be more comfortable—it is a psychological thing and not anymore purely rational. These kinds of considerations are what my work revolves around. There's an infinite, ever-changing potential within those most common, mundane things.

FB   I'd like to come back to the *Panorama* exhibition. It was loosely divided into three chapters: *Life Space*, *Work Space*, and *Public Space*. What was interesting about the exhibition concept is that when one thinks of Konstantin Grcic, one tends to think

Shawn Maximo, *Rest Stop*. Artwork for *PIN–UP*, 2014

CASSINA. THIS WILL BE THE PLACE

of individual pieces, not completely assembled environments. I simply can't imagine you as an interior designer developing spaces completely furnished by yourself.

KG   No, doing complete spaces never appealed to me so much. I think I am better at designing individual products than doing a whole interior.

FB   And yet you designed the *Life Space* for the exhibition, a sort of ideal-typical apartment that simultaneously seems a bit dystopian.

KG   Designing *Life Space*, as well as the other two environments *Work Space* and *Public Space*, was the deliberate choice to challenge my own routine. All three environments are conceived in a very conceptual way. Each one formulates a given theme: *Life, Work, Public*. I wanted the scenes to provoke a reaction from the viewer, whether it be positive or negative. In *Life Space*, for example, the room has a big window that looks out on to an airport. Some could say, "That's horrible! Who would want to live at the airport?" The truth is that the overpopulation and urban growth forces more and more people out toward the city's periphery and suburbs. Eventually, housing will sprawl out to the most unimaginable places like an airport.

That's the pessimistic reading of *Life Space*. The optimistic reading of it would be: "Fantastic! I live at the airport! I can go anywhere from here while others can easily reach me. And, I have a 24/7 infrastructure of restaurants and shopping—even a church and hairdressers." [Laughs.] I wanted to stimulate a certain ambiguity in the spectators, who would have to make up their own minds about what side of the story they wanted to see. Their discursive participation was an important incentive for the whole exhibition project.

FB   I got a whole different take on your design for the *Life Space* after reading the Sloterdijk text in the *Panorama* catalogue, which deals a lot with egosphere and in which he describes the modern apartment as architectural and topological analog of modern individualism. I also saw a lot of connections to Le Corbusier's Unité d'habitation.

KG   Le Corbusier's Unité d'habitation can be seen as a reaction to the changing lifestyles of its time. In fact, our generation is not nearly as confrontational or experimental or free in our thinking as they were back then. Admittedly, a lot of designs from that era have come to constitute a retro-modernist style, which makes us forget just how explosive these ideas were at

Konstantin Grcic, *Props accessories*, Cassina, 2016.
Playtime exhibition, Galerie Max Hetzler, Berlin

Le Corbusier, Unité d'habitation, Marseille, 1952

the time. I still get very inspired by it and feel that a lot of the issues that were raised then are still relevant today.

FB   To what extent do you include anthropological research into your own design process?

KG   Anthropology and sociology both provide the sustenance for design. The work of a designer always relates to people, and their lives. It's a great privilege, but it also imposes great responsibility. Knowledge is at the core of everything we do. In order to change things, we need to know better. Design is not about changing things for the sake of change. Design should not be imposing, but rather make an offering, a proposal. That's why I feel that small projects are good and effective drivers of change. Even if they don´t have big commercial penetration, they can still have an effect. There are so many famous examples. Think of the Memphis group that only existed for a very short time, producing mostly prototypes and one-offs. Still it had an enormous influence on designers around the world. Memphis, and other similar movements of the time, became a creative valve for growing social discontent. There was an urgency that also existed during the similarly creative times of Le Corbusier or the Bauhaus, and then again in the 1950s and '60s. The need for social change fertilizes a new form of design.

FB   Would you say that good interior design should definitely have a disruptive element?

KG   Yes. For me, there's something unnatural about interiors that are cast in one mold, where everything fits together perfectly. I'm finding that disconcerting. Interestingly, Le Corbusier was quite effective in creating small disruptions in his projects. Even though his interiors were perfectly staged, they always displayed an eclectic mix of things. For example, the beautiful curved *Thonet* chair, which is used in so many of his interiors, breaks with the industrial rigor of his architecture. Then, of course, he had a good sense for color that added an unexpected emotional aspect. These were deliberate disruptions that had a positive effect for the quality of the space.

FB   Which naturally begs the question: what does your own home look like?

KG   It's changing. I have a little family now, and that has created needs that never before existed [Laughs]. It's a whole new experience for me, but I like it. For the first time in my life I now live with a sofa. I never thought I needed one, which by the way explains why I have never designed one. Ours is a beautiful old two-seater sofa designed by Dieter Rams in the early sixties. It's funny how small it is compared to most sofas of

Konstantin Grcic, *Teepee* chairs, Cassina, 2008

View of Le Corbusier and Pierre Jeanneret's "L'Esprit Nouveau" Pavilion
at the Exposition Internationale des Arts Décoratifs et Industriels Modernes, Paris, 1925

Konstantin Grcic, *Soft Props* sofa, Cassina, 2017

today. That again says so much about how our lifestyles have changed and how furniture reflects those changes. Anyway, the small sofa is perfect for us and I feel embarrassed thinking how, for such a long time, I have been totally ignorant of the quality a sofa can have for a home.

FB   Are you more optimistic or pessimistic about the future of design and especially the future of residential design?

KG   Optimistic! Absolutely!

FB   Why?

KG   Design is an act of emancipation. While our life is subject to certain conditions, design enables us to change these conditions. It's empowering, that's why I am optimistic. And design isn't limited to the creation of objects, but first of all, it is a form of thinking, of thinking ahead.

KONSTANTIN GRCIC
Munich, Germany

Konstantin Grcic was trained as a cabinetmaker at The John Makepeace School in Dorset, England before studying Design at the Royal College of Art in London. Since setting up his own practice Konstantin Grcic Industrial Design (KGID) in Munich in 1991, he has developed furniture, products, and lighting for some of the leading companies in the design field. Many of his products have received international design awards such as the prestigious Compasso d`Oro for his *Mayday* lamp (Flos) in 2001, the *Myto* chair (Plank) in 2011, and the *OK* lamp (Flos) in 2016. Work by Konstantin Grcic forms part of the permanent collections of the world´s most important design museums, including MoMA (New York), and Centre Georges Pompidou (Paris). Konstantin Grcic has curated a number of significant design exhibitions such as *Design-Real* for The Serpentine Gallery, London (2009), *Comfort* for the St. Etienne Design Biennale (2010), and *Black2* [1] for the Istituto Svizzero, Rome (2010). In 2012 he was responsible for the exhibition design of the German Pavilion at the 13th Architecture Biennale in Venice [2]. Solo exhibitions of his work have been held at the Museum Boijmans Van Beuningen (Rotterdam, 2006), Haus der Kunst (Munich, 2006), The Art Institute of Chicago (2009), the Vitra Design Museum (Weil am Rhein, 2014) and the Kunsthalle Bielefeld (2016). The Royal Society for the Encouragement of Arts, Manufactures and Commerce (RSA) appointed Konstantin Grcic "Honorary Royal Designer for Industry (Hon RDI)"; in 2010 he was fellow at Villa Massimo in Rome. Design Miami awarded him the title "2010 Designer of the Year" and in 2016 he was awarded the Personality distinction for his achievements by the German Design Council.

|1|

|2|

BEATRIZ COLOMINA

Architectural historian, theorist, and curator Beatriz Colomina has been stirring up international architectural discourse for nearly thirty years. A professor at Princeton University, the Spanish-born scholar has written and edited many highly acclaimed and provocative books and essays that analyze, among other themes, how questions of war, sexuality, and mass media affected the production of architectural space over the course of the twentieth century. As for the twenty-first, Colomina has proclaimed it the "century of the bed."

FELIX BURRICHTER   Your theory of the "century of the bed" is essentially that it's a postindustrial phenomenon that we see beginning in Europe and the US in the postwar period.

BEATRIZ COLOMINA   Yes. There have always been artists and writers that work in bed. Like Proust, notoriously, or Truman Capote in the postwar years, or Matisse. But what's characteristic of our time is that something that was supposed to concern only eccentric artists and writers now applies to everybody. And that shift is what I find fascinating, that now everybody is in bed, and everybody is an artist in a way. With the new media, we've all become authors of some kind. The new media facilitate the possibility of working in bed. I read today that just by being on Facebook, you're producing $36 a year for them—just for being there, before you even do anything! Even when you think you're relaxing in bed and booking your tickets for a Caribbean holiday, you're working, because you're producing data that is mined and used. So that's work, a new kind of work that you may not even be aware of. The condition of 24/7 culture that Jonathan Crary talks about [in his book *24/7: Late Capitalism and the Ends of Sleep*, Versobooks, 2013] is very related to this question. He doesn't actually spell

it out, but it's obvious that the location of that kind of 24/7 work is the bed. He put what looks like an office building on the cover, the typical image of the twentieth-century city that never sleeps, but this image is already obsolete when many office buildings are empty and an army of dispersed but interconnected producers is working from bed.

FB   As you've said, the boudoir is taking over from the tower.

BC   Yes. There are many office towers in midtown Manhattan that are half empty even if they keep up appearances with all these security guys up front but when you go up entire floors are half empty. A lot of people in New York, particularly after 2008, aren't working in offices, they're in a much more dispersed condition, and, given the way most people live in New York in very small apartments, working from bed.

FB   So if you can now work in bed, does that mean more freedom?

BC   It would seem like more freedom, right? I don't have to get out of bed, I don't have to get dressed, I don't have to go the office. So in that sense it seems very attractive. But on the other hand, we all know how our lives have been changed by these new conditions. It used to be that you would go to work—to Princeton in my case—and when you came back home the school could call, they could even send a fax, but that was it. The students couldn't call you, they didn't have your number, it wasn't university policy. But now there's a barrage of emails at all times of the day and night about the paper that they're not writing, or the class they'll miss because of a dentist appointment, or the trip they can't come on because of a wedding. I don't care! So we have an overload of information and engagement, and everyone is taking advantage of it. I'll give you a really stupid example. When traveling for the university you used to put your receipts in an envelope and give it to the administrator in the office, and they would sort it out for you and reimburse you. But now you have to input everything yourself, scan all the paperwork, make sure you're following the rules of a very cumbersome system, and lo and behold you've wasted an hour of your life! So we're all working much more under these conditions, and we're all on 24/7. It's not that funny anymore, you know what I mean. It's good and it's not good. It's good that sometimes you don't have to to go to the workplace, but the information overload is really taking its toll on all of us.

FB This is making me think of *Playboy* founder Hugh Hefner's famous bed, which you've written about.

BC Yes, he had an extraordinary round bed, surrounded by equipment, which basically allowed him to become a voluntary prisoner of architecture or, as he put it himself, "a contemporary recluse." That's what he told Tom Wolfe, who came to interview him in bed—Hefner did interviews in bed long before John Lennon and Yoko Ono. He did everything in bed! Have you seen the pictures of him in bed surrounded by layouts, slides, pictures, tape recorders, projectors, candy bars, Pepsi cans, etc.? And there were so many phones in that bed, and filing cabinets and fridges and all kinds of things.

Hugh Hefner's bedroom photographed by Mario Bellini in 1972

Henri Matisse as he works on the decoration for Chapelle du Saint-Marie du Rosaire in Vence from his bed in his room at the Hôtel Régina in Cimiez, 1949

It's amazing all the equipment he had. He could control all the lights in the house from his bed. Everything. His bed became a control room.

FB But, as you say, he ended up becoming a prisoner of that, just as we are today.

BC Yes. New media open up new possibilities of working in different ways, so you have more freedom with respect to where you are, but at the same time you're also overloaded with information and it never stops. We all end up with attention-deficit disorders.

FB Is that what you call horizontal architecture?

BC The twentieth century was the century of the horizontal. Not just the century of the bed in the sense of working in bed, but also the century of the divan of Sigmund Freud, and of the chaise longue of tuberculosis patients at the beginning of the century—think of all these images of people with tuberculosis in modern buildings in the first half of the century. And the horizontality of modern architecture itself frames the view of this new position of the body. The figure of modernity, the paradigmatic client of modern architecture, is first the horizontal tuberculosis patient, and then the horizontal psychoanalytical patient, as TB gets under control with the discovery of streptomycin. This horizontal figure becomes dominant after the war, particularly in the US. It is not by chance that the postwar period brings the *Playboy* figure on the bed and produces a mass-market discourse about the bed and around the bed.

FB Now that we can basically lead our entire lives in bed—work, chat with friends, eat, sleep, have sex, etc.—the public and the private realms have collapsed into each other. Before, when you shut the bedroom door, it was private, but now it isn't anymore.

BC Yes, absolutely. It's a completely new condition. In the core of the most private space you are also totally exposed. And even when you don't think you're exposed, you are. All this data

being collected as you work-play, that's a form of exposure. You don't even realize it's happening. Some people are super careful and even put a Post-it over their laptop camera.

FB   I do that!

BC   Me too! But that deals only with one form of exposure. Look what we found out thanks to Edward Snowden. It's not just a commercial invasion of the private realm, a la Facebook, etc. It's also governmental. All this data collected ostensibly in the fight against terrorism. In reality it is about the erasure of the private.

FB   In your book *Domesticity at War* [MIT Press, 2007], you talked about how throughout the twentieth century achievements from the military-industrial complex gradually infiltrated the domestic realm. We're now entering a stage where the achievements of new media, which are also the result of military technology, have entirely infiltrated the personal and private realms. Is that the ultimate achievement of your theory of domesticity at war?

BC   I don't know if it's the ultimate achievement, but it's definitely another phase of that reality. There was already a lot about war in my earlier book *Privacy and Publicity* [MIT Press, 1994]. Even if it wasn't the main theme of the book, it argues that modern architecture came

out of World War I, and that the technologies that defined World War I became domesticated in the immediate postwar years. Radio and the telephone were crucial to the war, and entirely changed the way warfare was conducted. Before you had soldiers at the front, and the general was there too and could see when it was time to retreat. But then you had a new condition where the soldiers are at the front but the commanders-in-chief are in the rearguard, on their telephones, barking orders and sending people to their death without seeing the conditions on the ground. That's why it was the most violent war in history up to that point, because of radio and telephone. After the war, you find the radio in the middle of the living room. It became domesticated, and it radically changed the sense of what's private and what's public—now public news was coming right into the house, whereas before you had to go out to get the news. All these modern architects were themselves traumatized by the war and were in a way responding to it—I mean Le Corbusier was trying to convince the Voisin company, which had manufactured warplanes during the conflict, that it should use its factory to mass produce housing. That didn't work out in the end but Le Corbusier's Plan Voisin for Paris has that name, because the company was the main sponsor. So what actually happened in the United States after World War II, with the transformation of the war industries into peacetime manufacturers—you know, armaments factories started making washing machines or lipsticks as Donald Albrecht demonstrated in his beautiful exhibition [*World War II and the American Dream*, National Building Museum, Washington D.C., 1994-95]—is something that Le Corbusier had already imagined in post-World War I France. War is written all over modern architecture right from the early years. It took a particular turn after World War II because, unlike many of the European architects in the First World War, the Americans were working for the military machine during the conflict. I mean Le Corbusier was always inspired by the military but not directly involved in World War I, unlike colleagues such as Walter Gropius, but many American architects were directly involved in the war effort during World War II and came back from the war with all these new techniques and ideas. The Eameses, for example, or Paul Rudolph, were experimenting with all these great new materials and new ways of building that had been developed during the war with money from the military. After the war you had the capability of doing something entirely different. So war is present in both early modern architecture and in the postwar years. It is even why domestic space takes on such an incredible relevance right after World

War II. John Entenza, the editor of *Arts & Architecture* magazine who sponsored the Case Study houses in Los Angeles, wrote that men coming back from the war would no longer want to live in a traditional house with a picket fence and a pitched roof because they had become accustomed to modern machinery and would therefore demand modern architecture. That's a fascinating idea, if you think about it. He thought that the war had modernized the client, basically. And for a short period right after the war people were very interested in that. For example when Bucky Fuller did his Dymaxion House [first put forward in 1928 as the 4-D house and redesigned in 1945 in an aircraft factory], there were tons of people signing up for one, and it was Fuller who didn't deliver in the end. A few years later that completely stopped, people preferred a more conventional, Levittown kind of house.

FB   What's also interesting in the postwar period is this idea of the house as a shelter, in the sense of a shelter from attack, because of course America was still at war, first in Korea and then later in Vietnam, not to mention the nuclear arms race that was the Cold War. And you get Texan builder Jay Swayze presenting his design for an underground shelter at the 1964 World's Fair in New York.

View of Levittown, Long Island, 1947-51

BC   Yes. Swayze had been a military specialist, advising the military on chemical warfare, and after the war he became a contractor of luxury houses. It is interesting that in the US the government didn't take responsibility for shelters. This is so American! In Europe they had these big collective shelters that were built by the government or the municipality and were paid for by the state. In the US they gave you a pamphlet saying, "This is how you can build your shelter," and good luck with it! You were responsible for your own shelter. In *Playboy* you have funny cartoons of guys building their own shelter and saying to the nice girl next door, "In case of a nuclear attack, you can come into my shelter, but none of the other neighbors can." [Laughs.] Anyway, they distributed this little catalogue on how to build a shelter, and basically you were on your own. After Kennedy's speech on the Cuban missile crisis in 1962, it became very dramatic. And just two years later at the fair you have this guy, Swayze, who claims that it's much better simply to build your whole house underground, so you are already "sheltered." He says, "real windows are not important because we don't really look out of the window anymore. It's much better to have an artificial landscape and a view that you can change at will." You could have a night sky in the kitchen and a sunrise in the living room. You could have whatever—rain or a storm if you were in the mood.

FB   You know I think the word "shelter" is so interesting. Because you have the meaning we've just been talking about, in the sense of bomb shelters,

Karl Friedrich Schinkel, *Zeltzimmer*, Charlottenhof, Potsdam, ca.1830

A view of the underground house designed by Jay Swayze for Girard Henderson in Las Vegas, Nevada, second half of the 1960s

which, as we've seen, Americans took very seriously in the postwar era and decked out as mini versions of the perfect suburban home. And then you have the concept of "shelter magazines"—you know, *Architectural Digest* or *Beautiful Living* or whatever they're all called. And then you have the idea of shelter for migrants and refugees, which of course is especially relevant right now.

BC   Yes. What is shelter today? Recently I read an article in the European press where they were talking to refugees who'd just arrived in Europe. They asked them what the most important thing was for them once they'd made the crossing, and they all said that, after water and food, the most important thing was to charge their cell phone. None of them mentioned a bed or a house or a shelter in the traditional sense, they all said they needed their phones. So you could argue that the cell phone is a new form of shelter. They all come with their cell phones—in places like Izmir, they sell a whole kit to cross the sea, with a life vest and a whistle, but also these sort of condoms for the phones, because it's crucial that your phone works when you get to the other side. The most important thing to do on arrival is to get a SIM card, and to plug in the phone and connect. Because that's the only thing they have left—that's where the photographs of their loved ones are, that's where their contacts are, through social media, that's where they're getting all their information, their maps... They are sharing all kinds of information, but it is also their community. Everything. So this is shelter now. It's pretty intense. After World War I, the domestic interior

becomes dominated by the radio, after World War II it's invaded by television, but now the cell phone is a form of shelter.

FB   There's a complete dissolution between inside and outside, between interior and exterior.

BC   Yes. But what's more, the possibility of survival is in the cell phone. If you offer refugees a house or a bed on Lesbos, that's fine but ultimately that's not where they want to be. They want to move on and the phone is the instrument that makes it possible. The cell phone is exhibit number one of the conditions of our times. It's a new form of domesticity.

FB   If this is the new form of domesticity, how does it translate into the actual, physical spaces in which we live?

BC   I think what's interesting about our times is that we're now clearly living in a new kind of hybrid space that's both physical and digital. Back in 2000 there was no social media, but in the last fifteen years social media has changed the way we live so radically. And it's becoming more and more exacerbated. In Korea, for example, there's KakaoTalk, and 95% of the population is using it. Even grandmothers are on KakaoTalk—you cannot exist socially without it. It may be "virtual," but its societal effects are totally real.

FB   So digital space is now just as real as actual physical space. What effect does this have on aesthetics?

BC   It's interesting you should say that, because of course it does have an effect. For example, people do care what their telephones look like. In Istanbul, in particular, they're totally crazy about how their phones look. It's extraordinary. I mean presumably people aren't as wealthy there as here, but they all change their cell phones much more often so as to have absolutely the latest version. They're crazy about it! Cell phones of course have a whole aesthetics unto themselves, which is Bauhaus-based—Steve Jobs claimed to have been influenced by the aesthetics of the Bauhaus. But more and more people are becoming interested in this kind of minimalist form of existence and of architecture. So I think there's a relationship between the aesthetics of the cell phone and this renewed interest in more minimalist forms of architecture. I mean a few years ago you could buy a modernist house in the US for nothing. In Princeton, for example, there's a Marcel Breuer house, which had been shown at MoMA, and which is on a fantastic lot, and the first time I saw it, it was so cheap—it was being offered for something like $150,000, absolutely nothing! And a traditional, stupid house in Princeton, in the same location, would have sold for a lot more, like $500,000. But today many people want a modernist house. They have become difficult to find, even in Princeton.

FB   I also feel like there's been aesthetic influence from digital renderings—they've become so photo-realistic, but at the same time you can produce the most outlandish things.

BC   Yes. I was talking with my good friend the architect Andrés Jaque a few years ago and he mentioned how, in the middle of the crisis in Spain, he started taking little jobs from young people who wanted to renovate their apartments, and he said that now people don't ask what something ought to look like, rather they want to know how it will look as a background for Facebook or other social media. This is very interesting. In the early twentieth century, architects were accused of producing architecture that would only look good in photographs, and now at the beginning of the twenty-first century we have clients requesting that their architect produce a background that looks good on social media. Physical space has become a backdrop, a kind of stage, for social media. That's another kind of aesthetic.

FB   This is making me think of the 1964 World's Fair again which, for the most part, rather than being designed by big-name architects, was designed by corporations, with results that were rather garish, brash, loud, and, to some people's taste, kitsch. But probably it was all about what it would look like on TV—it was made to look like a commercial.

BC   Yes, and it was very popular with the public. The architectural critics were all up in arms, but popular critics loved it.

FB   "The dream of the future is technological, and the house/the home is its laboratory." That's a quote from the World's Fair. But if you think about the bedroom, the space where everything happens now, it hasn't really changed that much, has it?

Philippe Starck, *Privé* island, Cassina, 2008

Piero De Martini, *La Barca* model, Cassina, 1975

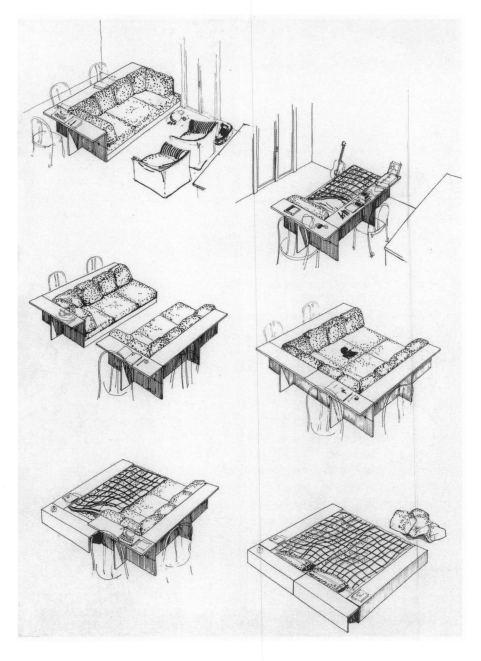

The versatility of the *La Barca* model by Piero De Martini, sketches

BC   But what about all these micro apartments that are now being built in New York? They are really just oversized bedrooms. That was unthinkable a generation ago! What's happening? There's a concentration: you walk into one of these micro dwellings and practically throw yourself onto a horizontal surface, because there is nothing else. That's the one parameter we don't seem to have been able to eliminate. Sleep. The military are working very hard on that one though. Did you hear about these studies they're doing on birds that are able to migrate for long periods of time without having any rest? They're looking very closely at the brains of these birds to see if they can figure out how to allow humans to go without sleep for two or three weeks. It would be very useful for warfare, of course, but before we know it this will be applied to all of us. The micro apartment is very much related to this. We no longer need so much physical space. That belongs to another era. Nobody needs all these books like I have here at home. Nobody has this many books anymore. But I also have a micro apartment in Princeton, which is 260 square feet, and I love that it's so small, no books, and I love it that the whole world is out there.

FB   So rather than the home being the laboratory of the future, have we ourselves now become that laboratory since the home has been reduced to just pretty much a bed?

BC   I think maybe the home is still the laboratory: the walls have moved in on us, but it's precisely this that has expanded our horizons enormously. The bed is not a refuge from the world. The bed floats in the world, travels everywhere and knows no secrets. If you want to hide you have to get out of bed.

BEATRIZ COLOMINA
Princeton, USA

Beatriz Colomina is an internationally renowned architectural historian and theorist who has written extensively on questions of architecture, art, sexuality, and media.

She is the Founding Director of the Program in Media and Modernity at Princeton University—a graduate program that promotes the interdisciplinary study of forms of culture that came to prominence during the last century and looks at the interplay between culture and technology—and Professor of History and Theory in the School of Architecture.

Her books include *Are We Human? Notes on an Archaeology of Design*, coauthored with Mark Wigley (Lars Müller, 2016) [1], *Manifesto Architecture: The Ghost of Mies* (Sternberg, 2014), *Clip/Stamp/Fold: The Radical Architecture of Little Magazines 196X-197X*, co-edited with Craig Buckley (Actar, 2010), *Domesticity at War* (MIT Press, 2007), *Privacy and Publicity: Modern Architecture as Mass Media* (MIT Press, 1994) [2], and *Sexuality and Space* (Princeton Architectural Press, 1992).

Together with Mark Wigley she is the curator of the 2016 Istanbul Design Biennial *Are We Human? The Design of the Species: 2 seconds, 2 days, 2 years, 200 years, 200,000 years*.

She has written numerous other publications and presented lectures throughout the world, including at MoMA, the Guggenheim and the Metropolitan Museum of Art in New York; the MAXXI museum in Rome, Museo Nacional Centro de Arte Reína Sofia in Madrid, MACBA in Barcelona, Tate Modern in London, MOCA in Los Angeles, Istanbul Modern, Neue Nationalgalerie in Berlin, The Samsung in Seoul.

are we human?

notes on an archaeology
of design

by

Beatriz Colomina
& Mark Wigley

Lars Müller Publishers

|1|

PRIVACY
AND
PUBLICITY

Modern Architecture as Mass Media

COLOMINA

|2|

ARNO BRANDLHUBER

In the context of the German construction industry, where *Ordnung* reigns supreme and rules and regulations are sacrosanct, Arno Brandlhuber is something of a rebel. The Berlin-based architect believes that to face today's demographic challenges—aging populations, increasing cultural diversity, and new modes of living that depart from the traditional family unit—fewer rules are needed, not more. With respect to the boundaries between inside and out, between public and private, and between architecture and design, the spaces of the future, he insists, are going to be more fluid and free.

FELIX BURRICHTER Let's talk about the future, Arno!

ARNO BRANDLHUBER Gladly. But if we talk about the future and how things will look, we need to think in various scales—from the overall geopolitical contexts down to the individual object. And there we come to the role of furniture. That is, if we think in this sort of "what is the future?" framework. The future has become more uncertain. Not to necessarily fall into a negative momentum, but I find it very helpful as background noise for such a discussion to look at what's happening politically in Europe. The Schengen project is in crisis, and many European countries are experiencing a swing to the right. Nation states want to define themselves more strongly again and are thus isolating themselves. So if we're going to talk about furnishings, then we should also talk about how the various countries and people within this "Europe" construct are furnishing themselves, figuratively speaking.

FB "Furnishing"—whether in the literal or figurative sense—always assumes a certain degree of security and stability.

AB Right. That's why arranging our future is very interesting as a theoretical concept. In Europe we're in a very privileged position, of course. But that privilege is being questioned, and there's a certain insecurity that's also carrying over into the role of objects and homes. What's happening is that this whole set of building regulations—norms, safety standards, drop heights, toppliness of chairs, risk of injury—is up for discussion. Even German politicians are urging that these strict building regulations perhaps be reviewed after all. Because otherwise we can't organize, can't build the many units now required—for example, to accommodate the incoming refugees. That means that this insurance moment, this self-insurance, this setting the standards ever higher so that we no longer hear our neighbors, no longer consume any energy because we packed so much insulation onto the facade—in other words, all these backdrops ultimately conceived out of a restriction—is floundering. And that will ultimately have consequences for design.

FB In other words: progress through regression?

AB Yes. Because we realize that the many regulations are making it increasingly difficult to access architecture as finished product, if for no other reason than that prices rise along with standards. This is a new way of thinking that's

Brandlhuber+Emde, ERA, Burlon, building located on Brunnenstrasse, Berlin, 2007–2010, view of the gallery

only now being considered, in part because of the immigration. The question is: how can we create new structures, new architecture to house the refugees? Clearly, only on the basis of lower standards than those we've hitherto set for ourselves. But if we take that seriously, it means we can also lower our own standards. This concept of protection as we now know it— whether in the form of heat insulation or national borders—no longer holds. That's why I've started to simply loosen the standards for all our projects, especially those in Berlin. Or at least define them less precisely. That doesn't mean, for example, that there's no more insulation or soundproofing. But it does mean that we differentiate according to the situation.

FB Can you cite some concrete examples of this type of architecture?

AB Our Brunnenstrasse building [2009-10] in Berlin is a good example of an architecture that's not yet completely defined. It's more raw on the surfaces, and the spaces are not yet fully defined—you don't know if it's a living room or work area. That has a lot to do with the furniture and the objects that make a room what it is. Space, in other words, is defined by temporal or temporary provisions. If, for example, there's a bed, then the space is what we'd typically identify as a bedroom or sleeping area. But you don't just sleep in a bed, to stick with this particular object. You also read, work, have sex. These are spatial co-organizations.

Compared to the Brunnenstrasse project, Antivilla [2015] is a double experiment because there was this existing structure of the old VEB fabric warehouse from the 1980s. When there's an existing structure, it always has value—regardless of whether it's a beautiful old design object or a horrible relic from the dump. Spaces live from the energy contained in these structures or objects, the energy of their creation, the muscle energy and so on. If one accepts that, then the next question is how to convert the existing material using as little additional energy as possible so that it once again opens up possibilities and assumes a form that can be used but that isn't predetermined.

It was precisely this question that arose during the design process for Antivilla. It was obvious that this new use of the space would also involve other people—that is, a larger group of people—since the building is much too large for my girlfriend and I and to use as a private weekend home. So we asked ourselves as a group how we could make this space our own with the goal of making something that seems immobile and unchangeable more fluid again. Take, for example, the original windows, which were very small and uniform. We said, "Here's a wall. It's closed. Behind it is the lake. I want to see the lake, so let's make a hole." Not windows in

a specific size. Not this determinism of the cut-out. But rather, an actual hole. Of course it also had a lot to do with Michel Piccoli in the movie *Themroc* [Claude Faraldo, 1973]—that way of working directly with the material. It's not a form of sophisticated design, of refinement, but rather the opposite. It's a directness, also with regards to expectations of what surfaces should look like that aren't immediately fulfilled. But then this multiple non-fulfillment produces a totally new space. And as we know from math, a double negative always makes a positive.

FB   Art is also very present in the Antivilla.

AB   Yes, there's a lot of art, most of it from friends for whom we've done something in the past. There's a chair by Matti Braun from the '90s located precisely at this intersection of design, object, and art. And a work by Karin Sander, a piece of framed woodchip wallpaper as big as one of the windows. On the floor, there's a work by Gregor Hildebrandt—magnetic tape glued together from old cassette tapes, which we then joined using epoxy resin. As for the furniture, we started to make a lot by ourselves, or to add simple things, like the pieces by Muller Van Severen, which are actually just wire frames. They don't assume specific functions until coverings or hard surfaces are added.

Brandlhuber+Emde, Burlon, Antivilla, Krampnitz, 2010–2015, view of the facade

FB   You mentioned that the Antivilla is more than just a private weekend home...

AB   Yes, there's always a lot going on. One day there might be a symposium or a workshop, and at the same time, a friend might stop by who wants to use the house for a day over the weekend, and so on. Originally, it was all one open space, but I've now conducted an intervention: I moved a 45 degree mirrored wall into one of the corners upstairs in order to create a private space where there's now a bed. Something very interesting is happening as a result; the corner has been mirrored away. You look in and, of course, look right back out again at a 90 degree angle. The room gets bigger, and at the same time, you've gained a private space. A true discovery!

FB   The term "hypercontextualism" is often used to describe your work. Brunnenstrasse and Antivilla are both excellent examples of your knowing how to "read" a very particular context in a very specific way, working with existing structure. But is there also something universal in the approach to each specific context?

AB   I find this contrast between hypercontextual and universal very interesting. Is the approach universal? Or is it first and foremost about the context, and not until the final product is something universal conveyed? For me, self-restriction is a kind of universal working method. That means limiting one's field of possibilities so thoroughly through the examination of all prescribed external conditions that there seems to be only one option available. Ideally,

Muller Van Severen, *Rack + Seat*, 2012

Bedroom designed by Adolf Loos in 1903 for Lina and Adolf Loos's apartment at Bösendorferstrasse 3 in Vienna, replica made for the *Ways to Modernism: Josef Hoffmann, Adolf Loos, and Their Impact* exhibition, MAK, Vienna, 2014–2015

the final product is then completely embedded in the context and at the same time completely liberated from it. Maybe this self-discovery in design can't be understood as something that one invents anew, as something unprecedented, but rather as intense self-restriction until something emerges borne with such inevitability that suddenly radiates something entirely different. And maybe that's how you gain something that could be described as universal.

FB   We've talked about how an existing structure affects spatial design. But to what extent does usage affect the determination of space and the various possibilities it offers for either working and living?

AB   I find it interesting when the orientation of the space isn't defined right away through the architecture, but rather when space takes on its proper form as a result of the way it's used. For that, you need a few tools, but often not many. The interior design of the walls and surfaces does not constitute one of these tools. They are located, rather, in objects—in other words, in the furnishings. The space isn't defined by the way it's used, but rather can make certain uses possible. At best, several uses. And through its furnishings, it can often take on various functions at the same time. I live in a situation, for example, where everything is bed-

room, everything is kitchen, everything is working space, everything is library, because there are no more walls at all.

FB   Do you consider that a form of luxury?

AB   Definitely. I've never had such a large bedroom, never had such a large kitchen. But it's not an open floor plan where there are still functional specifications. Instead, everything is superimposed in parallel. I think it's about keeping spaces much more fluid, more open, but also being able to close them when you want to—just not for ten years, or even twenty-four hours.

FB   Is this a kind of habitat that you create just for yourself? Or do you think this is the lifestyle of the future and that if everyone did this, we'd be much better off?

AB   Let's look at an entire city. The open model I'm proposing would avoid producing these socially homogenous situations where those from a lower socioeconomic context are crowded into the outskirts while the affluent claim the urban centers for themselves. In fact, it would all be totally mixed. Because that's exactly what makes the world livable. And as a result, for the first time, the city would perhaps become a pacified zone, one that can produce maximum het-

Brandlhuber+Emde, ERA, Burlon, building located on Brunnenstrasse, Berlin, 2007–2010, view of an interior

erogeneity—social, cultural, religious, ethnic. The question is: how far do we allow that model into our private spaces? Our own four walls, after all, are considered protected space, space that remains unharmed and supposedly also "unsurveilled." But that's not really true anymore anyway, because when we're on social media or, for example, when we google something, our personal data pops up everywhere. I think we can reproduce the same thing in spaces, and that would by no means be a degradation. But it doesn't mean you need an apartment that's cloistered, so to speak, in the same way only in order to then be connected back to the city via a hallway and stairwell, where you then enter yet another private sphere via a hallway and stairwell. Instead these transitions would become much more fluid.

FB   So in principle, the threshold is more interesting than the room?

AB   Yes. And yet the threshold still thinks between two different states. But if you now say, "it's *all* threshold, and I define it, and it can be shaped in the overall space of the toilet, the bed reaching out all the way to the city," then you have a completely different model. You no longer have this separation, where you differentiate between furnishing of public space or furnishing in private. It becomes a kind of open organism.

FB   Why is Berlin particularly well-suited as a research area for your work?

AB   It has something to do with the fact that Berlin was an insular situation before the fall of the Wall, a place where a lot of very different scenes came together, from those who avoided military service to various music scenes… and, of course, the squatters. That wouldn't have been possible in the same form in West Germany. Maybe we have to go back and specifically recognize these different generations of squatter movements. It's very interesting the way they renegotiated and legalized the term *Instandbesetzung*, the way one legally occupies an abandoned building through "rehab squatting." The second point is that Berlin was an extremely affordable city, which meant that many people from the cultural context came here. That, of course, resulted in this amalgam of artists, musicians, and a lot of architects who, unlike in expensive cities like New York, London, and Paris, didn't have to attain a very high level of monetary revenues in order to maintain their standard of living. Instead, they made much more use of the city, living at a relatively modest monetary level. That made all kinds of experiments possible.

FB   Do you think these residential experiments are also applicable in cities that don't have this very specific history of Berlin?

AB   Definitely. These questions about the appropriation of space and its flexible furnishing can be transferred anywhere, especially to cities where the price per square meter is much higher than in Berlin. It's more interesting when the spaces are not preordained, but when you ask yourself: what does a piece of furniture really do? What can it do?

FB   What kind of status does furniture have for you personally? Both as status symbol and utilitarian object?

AB   In the best case, furniture carries a story that makes it non-exchangeable like, for example, a chair by Studio Zanini I brought back from a trip to Brazil, or a Pierre Jeanneret chair we found on the roof of the High Court in Chandigarh. But fundamentally, it's increasingly about contemporaneity for me. Just as we're working here as architects in the now, I like designers working in the now, whose work reflects our

time, whether it's work by Konstantin [Grcic], Muller Van Severen, or Kazuyo Sejima. I recently discovered a great chair that's relatively unknown: the *Lima* that Jasper Morrison designed for Cappellini in 1995. You can sit quite comfortably in it. Actually, it's an outdoor folding chair, but I think you can place an outdoor chair indoors. I find it much more interesting when you no longer have to differentiate between indoor and outdoor furniture, between public and private. At best, a chair functions completely in that transitional space.

FB   Would you say that what you value in terms of furnishings has changed over time?

AB   Yes. In fact it's changing again right now. If I bought a chair today, for example, I'd buy thirty right away and put them everywhere. You use one as a clothes rack, another as a bedside table. Some you can group around a table; the rest stand around and you just wait and see.

Le Corbusier, Hôtel Particulier for A. Jeanneret, color photograph of the living room, from *L'Architecture Vivante*, Fall 1927

Brandlhuber+Emde, ERA, Burton, building located on Brunnenstrasse, Berlin, 2007-2010, the facade overlooking the street

You can slide them together sometimes or arrange them in threes. Or not. To some extent, that raises the question: what are the ideal objects of the future? They should make something possible. Do something. Make something easier, whether it's sitting or whatever. But they shouldn't be so fixed, because the spaces in which we live no longer are either. Just as room typologies are dissolving, so too are categories of furniture.

ARNO BRANDLHUBER
Berlin, Germany

Arno Brandlhuber works as an architect and urban planner. He studied Architecture and Urbanism at the Technische Universität Darmstadt and the Accademia di Belle Arti in Florence.

From 1992 on, he initiated several project and office partnerships, with Zamp Kelp and Julius Krauss, and later on with Bernd Kniess (b&k+), among others. During this period, projects such as Neanderthal Museum (Mettmann, 1996) and the Kölner Brett (Cologne, 2000), as well as numerous publications, have been realized.

He is the founder of brandlhuber+ (2006) and Brandlhuber+Emde, Burlon; a collaborative practice with Markus Emde and Thomas Burlon based in Berlin since 2009. The projects during this period include the Haus Brunnenstrasse 9 (Berlin, 2009), the Antivilla (Krampnitz, 2014), and St. Agnes (Berlin, 2015). Arno Brandlhuber teaches at several universities and colleges. Since 2003 he has held the chair of architecture and urban research at the Academy of Fine Arts, Nuremberg and is directing the nomadic masters program: a42.org. He was a guest teacher at several universities including Technische Universität Wien, ETH Zürich, and Harvard Graduate School of Design. Besides his building practice he is researching the spatial production of the Berlin Republic, to which he has devoted several exhibitions and a recently published book entitled *The Dialogic City: Berlin wird Berlin*.[1] In addition he deals with the subject of "the legislative" in architecture as a determining factor in both his building practice as well as an architecture-theoretical discourse.

His practice has been included in the 9th, 10th, 11th, 13th, and 15th Architecture Biennales, with the latter featuring the collaborative film *Legislating Architecture* by Arno Brandlhuber + Christopher Roth.[2]

|1|

|2|

ZHAO YANG

The subtle, delicate work of Chinese-born architect Zhao Yang stands in sharp counterpoint to the megalomaniacal urban developments that often characterize contemporary Chinese cities. After studying in Beijing and at Harvard, Yang settled in the rural province of Yunnan, where he is honing an architectural approach focused on local craft and sustainable materials. His buildings seek a genuine sense of place through the incorporation of tradition, moving forward into a more ecologically responsible future for architecture.

FELIX BURRICHTER You moved back to China shortly after graduating from Harvard's Graduate School of Design. Did you ever consider working in the United States?

ZHAO YANG I could have applied for a job at a firm, but I actually never thought about this option, even before I went to the US. After I started at Harvard, I felt more and more strongly that I didn't belong. I felt more and more clear about my identity in a very different cultural setting. If I was going to work as an architect in the US I would have had to work for someone else. That wasn't appealing to me.

FB So much is said about a global culture, yet as you were exposed to a new place, you were reminded of your roots and background.

ZY That's the right way to put it, and it worked both ways. I was opening my mind to different people and ways of thinking, while being made aware of my own culture's potential. I felt I could really do something with it.

FB What do you think that potential is?

ZY I think the way to look at this discipline is basically different in the Chinese mind. Architecture is not heroic and it is non-object. It is just a background for the environment, it's a living environment. Only because of globalization has mainstream thinking been an influence— great buildings, a great opera house, and so on. People have become more interested in just the object, which might make no sense at all.

FB With the increasing wealth in China, do you think people have been overly focused on Western status symbols?

ZY Yes, that started in the 1980s when China opened up. People started to look to the West as the standard. That is how Chinese cities are built now.

FB So you didn't just go back to China, you moved to Dali Prefecture, in Yunnan Province. What led to that decision?

ZY Dali has become quite unique in recent years. I discovered that in 2011, one year before my graduation. A friend of mine from Beijing invited me to see a piece of land where she wanted to make a house. That became our first project there. That's also when I first thought of Dali as a place for possibly starting a practice. What's interesting there is that you can feel the energy, the free energy of a lively local community. It's not like Beijing or Shanghai—society in the big cities is controlled by the current system. It works according to a designed program and leaves very little possibility for architecture to contribute any significance to real life experiences. But Dali is not a political or economical machine. The new immigrants have moved here for a more balanced life. And the local society has remained agricultural in a traditional way. The landscape has still maintained a balance between the natural and the artificial. I would like my practice to deal with this kind of reality.

FB   Is the tourism a recent phenomenon?

ZY   In the last few years Dali has become very popular. They made a movie with Dali as the background, and recently Dali has become crowded, though most tourists are still Chinese. The local farmers are quite happy, for they have their households. They actually have more human rights than the citizens in Beijing because they own a piece of land. In the design and the policies of the CCP, they leave more flexibility in the countryside. The environment is well kept

and it becomes attractive to the people from the big cities. They come to rent or buy a piece of land to build a house or a hotel and try new ways of life.

FB   When the project that originally brought you to Dali fell through, what kept you there?

ZY   I like rural China much better than urban China. The spatial structure of Dali is still made of villages that are not dictated by any master plan, and many of my new projects take place in these settings. Eventually I started to feel that I have the opportunity to pick up a tradition that was broken for historical reasons, the societal transformations since the 1900s, or even earlier. After the end of the Qing dynasty [1644–1912], there was a drastic change over a hundred years, and I think Chinese civilization barely survived all those wars, movements, and cultural revolutions. If it still survives anywhere, it's in rural China, where it is still agricultural. And the basic spatial order still remains. I feel architectural practice can be more related to humanity and tradition here in rural China. And Dali can become an example of this great potential.

Zhaoyang Architects, Chaimiduo Farm Restaurant and Bazaar, Dali, 2016, view of the courtyard

Zhaoyang Architects, project for Lee's Residence, Pu'er, 2014–2017, rendering of an interior

FB   How do you as an architect avoid falling into an idealization of rural life and the agricultural vernacular?

ZY   It's really our clients who started this experiment of the contemporary lifestyle in rural China. This has to do with their contemporary needs as contemporary people. The starting point is not nostalgia, it's not like we want to bring the past back to the foreground. We have a whole lot of real problems to deal with. Sometimes we use vernacular materials only because they suit the situation. We might be the first generation in China who enjoys the freedom or confidence to behave in this manner. A hundred years ago the avant-garde intellectuals claimed that the whole Chinese tradition should be abandoned and you should only read Western books. From that point the country has been moving toward another extreme, and the people who govern this country have been putting things on a more disastrous course. Luckily the root of this culture is just too stubborn to be destroyed. It's very profound, and still exists in the subconscious of most people brought up in this culture. We have no choice but to be aware of it and only then can we be confident to construct our own way of life and be comfortable with it.

FB   I think a lot of what you do creates a balance between rural and the urban, the aspects of modern living.

ZY   I take that as a compliment. In the end, it's only possible to imagine architecture that provides pleasure for modern people, which we all are. And architecture can influence how the modern mind encounters natural phenomena and finds peace and delight in them. I also think the word "balance" makes sense in my work, because when we design a project the thinking happens on multiple levels. We never attack a problem individually. When we sense problems, we put them together. The thinking happens on different levels at once. There are hierarchies, but not in a linear manner.

FB   Would you say your design for the Shuangzi Hotel is a good example of this integrated approach?

ZY   Yes. I think so. We discover our architectural means by trying to understand the order of things in a place that gives it form, movement, and rhythm. Shuangzi Hotel is unique among our works also because of its construction method. The plan of the hotel is on two pieces of land that belong to two families. We had to design two buildings that work as one single hotel, to deal with the relationship between the two buildings, to make them separate but still feel like a whole. The setting is very rough, and the wind is strong, especially on the northern part of the site. In Dali, the altitude is high and the air is dry, so it feels cold to be without sunshine. However, being exposed to sunshine isn't

View of the Ou Yuan garden in Suzhou

agreeable either. So we have to modulate the sunshine by architectural means. The sketch started from the smaller piece of land in the north. The rocky cliff behind the site casts big shadows onto the northeast corner of the land, so we created a triangular courtyard to cut the site in two. The part at the waterfront is planned to be guestrooms and enjoys the view and more sunlight. The leftover triangle part of the building was planned as a restaurant and faces westward to receive sunshine after noon. And we have this pitched roof sloping towards the rocks so that the gesture of the buildings also opens up to catch more sunlight. The oblique axis of the triangle extends to the bigger piece of land in the south and becomes a corridor facing the cliff. A single, sloped roof that faces the other way becomes a gesture to protect the building from getting too much sunshine from the west. It's very rational. It starts from this very straightforward response to the site restraints, using timber because it is light—a cheap, local wood. It's soft pine. The color goes well with the rock. Using the wood is a very straightforward choice. We have carpenters in the Dali region who still know the local and traditional way of making timber pitched roofs. Fewer and fewer may be using that skill, but you can still find these carpenters. The result is then very basic and almost archaic.

FB How does this local building technique impact the construction?

ZY It worked so differently from the routine of our building industry. We couldn't even make construction drawings before the timber system was put together on the site. And the idea of control and precision was also shifted. When they saw the wood, for example, one column would be thicker than another or one beam a little warped. And the design had to provide tolerance for this kind of situation. Chinese culture is more relaxed in these situations. It's about being flexible and enjoying this life. In Japan it is more about pursuing a standard or certain level of perfection. But why does everything always need to be perfectly straight?

FB How is the philosophy of the design, which is so in sync with the building methods, translated to the interior, the furniture?

ZY Well, in the Dali region, the interior and exterior are not clearly divided. When we have stones we just expose them, from outside in. And most of the timber will be exposed, a rustic feeling of living. It's very simple and straightforward. Unfortunately, the construction of this project has been stopped for two years, we can only imagine the furniture to be very simple and archaic in form, with a limited material palette

CASSINA. THIS WILL BE THE PLACE

and handmade appearance. In Dali, carpenters make very simple, beautiful furniture out of wood.

FB Your design for a private home in Zhu'an is based on the classic topology of the Chinese courtyard house, not unlike the one you said you grew up in Chongqing.

ZY Well, they are actually related. I spent my childhood in a courtyard house. The whole intricate spatial and social structure of that Chinese vernacular environment taught me all the basics of being Chinese. I still remember running in all the alleys, corridors, and verandas of these courtyard complexes as a kid. It wasn't as clean as the Xizhou house, not as white. But I think there's the same feeling of moving around in a labyrinth. If you go one direction you go to one house, and then another house, and then you go another direction and you find a way back. During this process you can experience a very complicated series of spaces, a subtle relationship between inside and outside. It's a very clear memory, a very strong seed in my mind.

FB Would you say the Xizhou residence is a luxury home?

ZY If we define luxury by how much we satisfy the need of a domestic life, I would say it's luxury. But it's not extravagant. You have a lot of possibilities in this house, a lot of spaces for

"loitering." Especially for a man like my client, who's been trained as a traditional Chinese painter and calligrapher. He grew up in that culture and understands how to enjoy a house with courtyard gardens.

FB You didn't have to do a lot of explaining?

ZY My first proposal ended up being exactly what they were looking for. Geoffrey Bawa, the godfather of Southeast Asian architecture, was a very important inspiration for me. Last year I went to his house in Colombo, Sri Lanka and it was a courtyard house. I was attracted to that, and when I met these clients I showed them the plan of that house and explained, "This is what I am going to give you." Of course the two houses are different in complexity and spatial experience, but the fact that they are organized around a series of exterior spaces is quite similar. It's something visual I could give to my clients before signing the contract.

FB Do you think the particular typology of this house works well in a rural area, or can it also translate to a more urban environment?

ZY I think both. Have you ever heard of Suzhou? It's famous for its private gardens. Suzhou is very close to Shanghai. If you visit you will see well-preserved traditional Chinese gardens. Many Chinese people are proud of this garden tradition. It's an important tangi-

Zhaoyang Architects, Zhu'an Residence, Dali, 2015–2016, view of the garden courtyard

Zhaoyang Architects, Shuangzi Resort, Dali, 2012

ble tradition in China. These gardens are part of urban houses. Suzhou is a city. If you have a piece of land in the city and you don't want to make a shop, you just erect a wall. You can do whatever you want behind it. The Chinese way of living is very introverted. The typology in Suzhou is quite similar to the one we used in Xizhou. Courtyard houses can be found anywhere in China. Psychologically people want to face inside, not outside. This is the mindset when building a house in this culture. Dali is very windy, and the introverted quality makes even more sense here. The sun is very strong as well, so it's better to let it reflect on a white wall instead of having large windows.

FB The house in Pu'er is quite the opposite, it's quite open.

ZY Pu'er is a place with an almost tropical climate, but it's not hot because it's 1,300 meters above sea level. The climate in Pu'er is very pleasant—never hot in the summer and never that cold in the winter. You can enjoy the outdoors most of the year. My client was a woman who fought her way from a village deep inside the mountain. She is now established as a successful developer and made her fortune. She was not raised in the courtyard culture, so I provided her with an open plan, a free plan that faces a garden. As a result of the climate, open gardens, instead of enclosed gardens are typical in the region.

FB   How did they find you, or you them?

ZY   She was my first local client from rural Yunnan. The others were immigrants from big cities, a background that we were familiar with. She met a friend of mine at a yoga class. When she mentioned that she had a piece of land and wanted to build a house, my friend told her about me. And when they went to another resort to spend their holiday together there was a magazine in the hotel room that mentioned my work with Rolex. That's what convinced her.

FB   And how did you sell your design?

ZY   The proposal I delivered was very straightforward. It's an honest response to the site and the brief. It's not about taste, but the site conditions and how to take advantage of them. I presented a set of sketches for the plan and a massing model and she immediately accepted. It's what she wanted.

FB   You say that the furniture is the focus of the interior of the house. Was this furniture supplied by the client, or was it specifically bought or designed for this house?

ZY   Furniture is critical for the house because it suggests the program in an open fluid space. Currently they are still working on the construction for the interior. The client is also starting to be fond of well-designed modern furniture. But for this we still need to be patient. In that region of Yunnan province, rich families tend to buy redwood furniture from local craftsmen. It is ridiculously heavy and heavily decorated.

FB   Where do you see your practice, and architecture in general, going in the next ten or twenty years?

ZY   Twenty years would be a little too far away to anticipate. I guess that my current interest in architecture related to lifestyle and nature will remain as one focus. And I'm starting to have opportunities to try different types and scales of projects in different parts of China. I enjoy the geographical diversity and cultural depth of this country and it's not easy to get bored in a fast-changing China. But generally, I would like to imagine a non-object future of architecture.

FB   Do you see a more general approach to architecture, in the way you approach your projects, as a return to certain values that are very specific to the context?

Zhaoyang Architects, Shuangzi Resort, building the roof

ZY Yes. Architecture can only be discussed within a context. I don't believe that architecture has its essence or ontology for architects to pursue. What we happen to call architecture is just formed by whatever is not architecture. We enjoy the process of building up a rich understanding of a place and its people, then providing something that looks as if it grew there naturally. In the end, architecture is just a bunch of interrelationships. As stated by Chogyam Trungpa, "Art involves relating with oneself and one's phenomenal world gracefully." And this is the only interesting approach for me.

ZHAO YANG
Shuangzi, China

Zhao Yang is an architect. Born in Chongqing, China, he studied at Tsinghua University in Beijing, then established his own practice, Zhaoyang Studio, in 2007. For the first three years, the studio worked closely with Standardarchitecture, a leading new-generation design firm, in Beijing. Zhao was awarded the 2010 WA Chinese Architecture Award from Beijing-based *World Architecture* magazine. In the same year, he attended the Harvard Graduate School of Design where he received a Master's degree in Architecture with distinction. After graduation, Zhaoyang Architects moved to Dali, Yunnan Province. From a series of experimental projects such as Shuangzi Resort, Sunyata Hotel in Dali Old Town [1] and Zhu'an Residence, the practice tries to explore architectural solutions to the emerging Chinese urban and rural conditions and relate architecture to a tangible social, cultural, and natural background, a tradition that's been long forgotten by the contemporary design and building industry in China.
In 2012, Zhao was selected as the inaugural architectural protégé of the acclaimed Rolex Mentor and Protégé Arts Initiative. Under the direction of his mentor Kazuyo Sejima, Zhao designed Home-for-All in Kesennuma [2] to help victims of the Tohoku earthquake and tsunami in Japan.
Zhao's design works and interviews have been widely published. He has been invited to speak at Tshinghua University, Tongji University, Chinese University of Hong Kong, Tohoku University, and the Geoffrey Bawa memorial lecture, among others. In 2015, Zhaoyang Architects participated in the exhibition *From the Asian Everyday* at Toto Gallery Ma in Tokyo.

|1|

|2|

MARTTI KALLIALA

Martti Kalliala is a Finnish-born, Berlin-based architect whose work focuses on the relationship between technology, built form, and social innovation. He designs, writes,
consults, collaborates, and exhibits with/at/for a wide variety of institutions, media,
and commercial entities. These include, among others, the Guggenheim Museum, *Harvard
Design Magazine*, and *Flash Art*. He is also a founding member of the internationally per-
forming "xperienz design" group Amnesia Scanner.

HOW WE LIVE TOMORROW.
A POSSIBLE ANTHOLOGY

Since the beginning of mankind, humans have imagined what the future would look like. What kind of lives will we lead? What kind of transportation will we use? What will our dwellings look like? Our homes, our furniture, the objects we use and surround ourselves with? Ever since the industrial revolution, technology has played an important role in how scenarios for the future, are imagined, both enthusiastically embracing technological process as well as staunchly rejecting it. And yet most future fantasies imagined by humans, whether utopian or dystopian in nature, never quite happened as they were imagined. Or maybe they did, and we are already living in the midst of them without even noticing? The modern information age makes anything seem possible, and yet nothing is quite what it seems. Here Martti Kalliala speculates on a number of scenarios of what might or might never happen. Or do they already exist?

When Pinterest Becomes Form

A tabula rasa, a blank canvas, a carte blanche; whatever material the home was originally constructed of, its interior surfaces have now been washed out into a pure, matte white. Except for the glass of the windows no nook or cranny has escaped a brush soaked in perfect RAL 9010 latex paint. The home has become a white cube, where "interior design" and "furnishing" have been replaced by "curation." These domestic spaces are occupied by sparse arrangements and assemblages of affective objects, to be reconfigured or completely redone in a cycle of four to twelve weeks. Not primarily to be lived in, or to be used, but to be mediated, contemplated, and consumed as images.

Liberated from a pledge to utility—to be useful—these spaces surpass the beauty of any abode of today: In the corner a *Shanzhai* version of a Grcic chaise longue (its label tab says *Aquascutum*), on the wall a curved 64-inch screen playing a video loop of a greenish fire that surprisingly also emits heat; in the middle of the room a small, Andrea Branzi-esque, softly textured sculpture that doubles as a cat tree. A Turkish Angora cat in the exact color of the lounge chair sits on a window sill; next to the kitchen on a white plinth a composition of avocados, gracefully decayed apples, and fist-sized clumps of compressed crystalline e-waste sit on a 3D-printed kintsugi ceramic dish. A white grand piano, thirty pieces of the same chair arranged in an order verging on chaos, a stuffed coyote, and a fifteenth-century Gobelin: The insta(ll) shots look simply amazing.

This incessant circulation of objects wouldn't be possible without the development of a vast supporting infrastructure. Indeed, the outskirts of the city have become cities for objects. Big box retail stores along ring roads are flanked by cloud storage facilities housing the furniture, books, art, household objects, ephemera, and sometimes plain junk, that was formerly stored inside homes. In fact, most things acquired from the big boxes are stored directly into the "cloud" without first passing through a home. As in data centers, packets are deposited and retrieved day and night as curator-decorator-inhabitants mix and match—"juxtapose" and "negotiate"—objects and meanings on their screens at home and simply file in their orders.

Martti Kalliala, *When Pinterest Becomes Form*, 2017, digital collage, 23.5 x 31 cm (9 ¼ x 12 ¼ in)

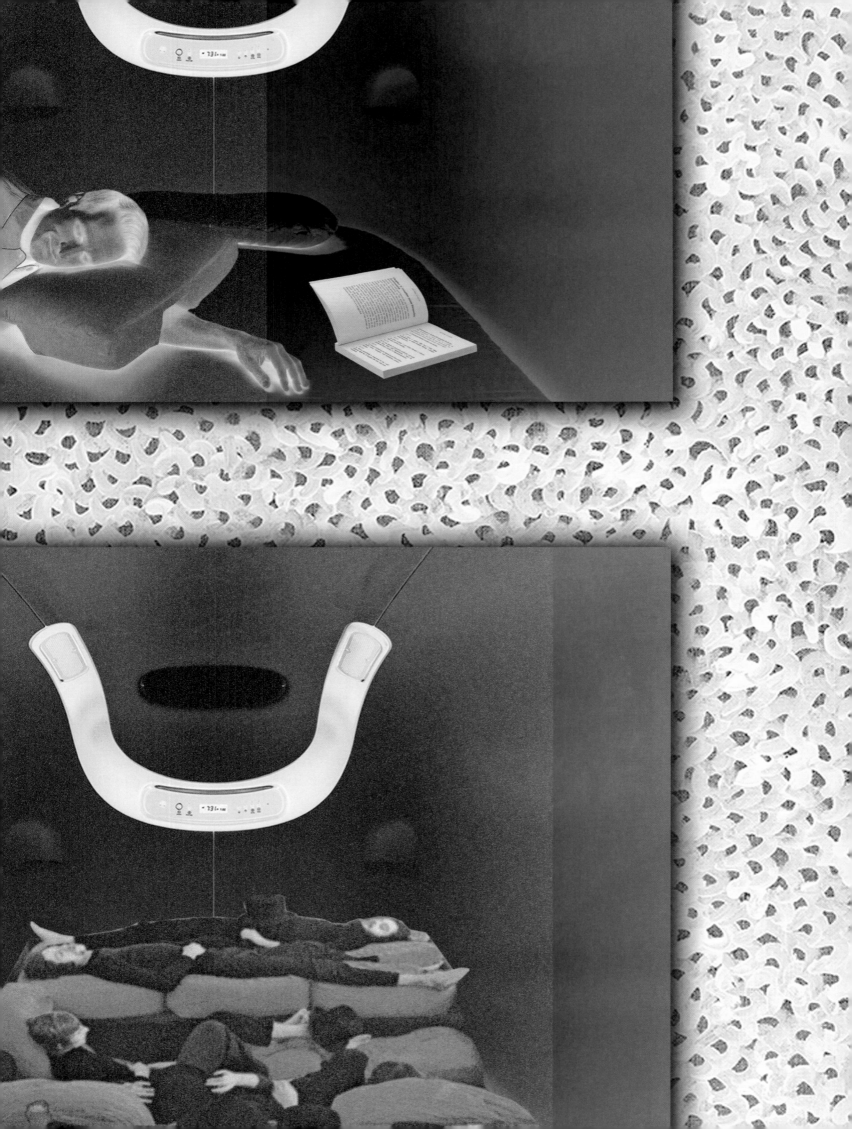

Together Forever

Across the urban world, real estate prices keep rising, ultimately curbing the entry of generations Y and Z to the housing market once and for all. Occupants might own a share of their shared home—most likely not—but at its core the dwelling isn't anymore considered property but a service. Occupants live with their #fam, phyle, thede, creche, polypool, smart contract family, FAOS (functional arrangement of strangers), or cloud community gone IRL. Correspondingly it is a widely held belief that the nuclear family and its associated single family home was nothing but a historical anomaly.

Liberated from the possibility of ever owning one's home, one is allowed to rethink the foundational concept: a safe space, welfare hotel, incubator, or a boarding house 2.0 catering to one's chosen lifestyle and associated journey of self-development. Some co-living units offer slow food jams, CrossFit revivals, and Pickling 4 Preppers seminars while *The Coming Insurrection* reading groups gather in the common room, where they'll find a military-grade Vitamix, a sofa for seven, and a gas stove in the shared kitchen. Other shared homes are structured around more austere, socially disciplined forms of life akin to what one might describe as a secular monastic order.

Individual rooms, cells, and pods differ greatly from house to house in size, shape, and design, but what they tend to have in common is an obsession with the bed—the locus and platform for work, rest, procreation, and education. From eleven-layer futons to czar-sized Hästens in Yayoi Kusama patterns to artisanal weighted blankets with embroidered inspirational motifs, co-living service providers respond to the ever-changing needs and desires of a new class of connoisseurs of horizontal existence.

This bubble collectivity has a huge spillover: cities incrementally become archipelagos of micro-cities, some in the scale of individual buildings, others of whole districts, each exhibiting a particular model—architecture, economy, culture, and aesthetic—of how to live together. Soon enough these islands begin to mushroom: many upmarket homes are distributed transnationally across a number of cities which themselves begin to transform into sovereign "zones." Re-coded forms of urban customer-citizenship arise; a distributed e-residency, urban elite members club, recognized across a variety of globally distributed federations, unions, and alliances of "smart" city-states enclaves: Muji X eStonia, Swissport, Candy&Gandhi, Alphabet Cities.

Martti Kalliala, *Together Forever*, 2017, digital collage, 23.5 x 31 cm (9 ¼ x 12 ¼ in)

Disruption Began At Home

On the 52nd floor of 420 Park Avenue in the exclusively solar-powered *Gigacity Midtown N-clave*, a home lies unoccupied. Swarms of Roomba vacuums tirelessly keep all surfaces clean while autonomous repair bots wage a slow battle against entropy. No one has ever lived in this dwelling and likely no one ever will. In fact its interior air is completely devoid of oxygen and consists solely of nitrous oxide to keep the furniture and collections of early twenty-first-century art (including many precarious installations) intact. The only purpose of this home—and the other 98 directly above and below it—is to function as a repository of value.

Some feel a bit uneasy about these empty shells of buildings and their artificially intelligent ghost inhabitants. Yet the same alien others have become widespread flatmates as the "smartness" of one's home has become an expected, default feature. Every device, surface, and object speaks to each other in a silent machine language coordinating their efforts to manage one's home. The popular KonMari™ AI smart home module has only a single goal: to unclutter. Its blind insistence on this task tends to make inhabitants anxious as sometimes it seems it would do whatever it takes to reach this goal, including disposing of its owners. But then again, never in the history of mankind have human dwellings been as spotlessly clean and uncluttered as today. On the other side of the world another home of a much more modest stature lies unoccupied; then suddenly a four person family moves in only to be replaced by a start-up nine days later, to be replaced after three months by 40 tonnes of raw aluminum that will stay there for the following three years. As it happens, under certain circumstances, the concept of "home" does not refer to any sort of permanent residence but one out of multiple uses attributable to any built space. Space itself has become a liquid asset, its functions, inhabitants, and material flows auctioned, traded, and speculated on the AIRBNX marketplace, thus most new construction adheres to the principles of infinite flexibility. A "home" is only one of the possible profit generating concoctions that can flow through space.

Martti Kalliala, *Disruption Began At Home*, 2017, digital collage, 23.5 x 31 cm (9 ¼ x 12 ¼ in)

Ageless (But Not Young)

Both rapid advances in biotechnology and the widespread adoption of the design principles laid out by the Reversible Destiny Foundation in their Bioscleave House (a house built as a machine for living forever) have led to the emergence of almost-non-senescent inhabitants that occupy their homes seemingly forever—at least from the perspective of those who choose to live as organic non-GMO humans. Those luckier ones who in the early 2000s rented apartments in coveted turn-of-the-nineteenth-century buildings might be enjoying the perks of rent control well into their 130s.

These homes—affectionately nicknamed *mausoleums*—have been retrofitted with uneven floors (to keep one alert) and a variety of vertical and horizontal bars, handles, grips, ropes, slings, and rings (to stimulate movement) that have seemingly replaced anything traditionally understood as "furnishing." Both aesthetically and functionally they are a curious mix of calisthenic park, BDSM playground, and the activity interiors built for primates exhibited in zoos, where limber ageless-but-not-young bodies swing from room to room. The 3-D landscape of the house, in combination with the body's friction, produces an aesthetics of resistance to corporeal complacency...

Martti Kalliala, Ageless (But Not Young), 2017, digital collage, 23.5 x 31 cm (9 ¼ x 12 ¼ in)

Kinvolk

The widespread longing for an #exit—an escape to an outside or elsewhere—assumes a variety of forms. Those with the means surf the market and change homes and living situations on a whim, others move to tower blocks built into airports being jurisdictionally and psychologically forever "in transit." Others decide to leave altogether.

Outside cities, in the woods of the Pacific Northwest, Scandinavia, Western China, and the Japanese Alps live a people known as *kinvolk*. A generation fed on aspirational imagery pertaining to authenticity, community, and "real experiences," where everything is craft and elaborate organic breakfasts represent an escape from their precarious jobs in the creative industries and endless austerity measures, have decided to "go native," and leave the mid-twenty-first century behind.

Deep in the insta-worthy scenery of the forest, Le Corbusier's Cabanon, Ted Kaczynski's hut, and Thoreau's Walden are authentically replicated and modded to allow for other manners of inhabitation than that of the single male bachelor. Furniture reminiscent of the Shaker and *Autoprogettazione* traditions, driftwood assemblages, dried flowers, and the occasional flotsam of industrial civilization adorn the sensually austere interiors of these arcadian huts, creating the perfect post-information-industrial idyll.

Others are bothered by the kinvolk abandoning the future as it was supposed to be like, condemning them as neo-Luddites or hopeless romantics for an idealized past. But the kinvolk know that time and progress don't move forward as a unilinear arrow. Time—and with it culture—is a spiral: everything that once was will return, but in different form. The kinvolk know we will live tomorrow as we lived in the past—only differently.

Martti Kalliala, *Kinvolk*, 2017, digital collage, 23.5 x 31 cm (9 ¼ x 12 ¼ in)

This Will Be The Place

FREE FLOW

Rooms with no hurdles
in a space without bounds.
Like liquid in motion,
where life can unfold.

A convivial retreat that
embraces ideas and
the comfort of doubt.
In the pool of life
everything moves
and nothing is fixed.
Variation is making
a bigger splash.

CASSINA. THIS WILL BE THE PLACE

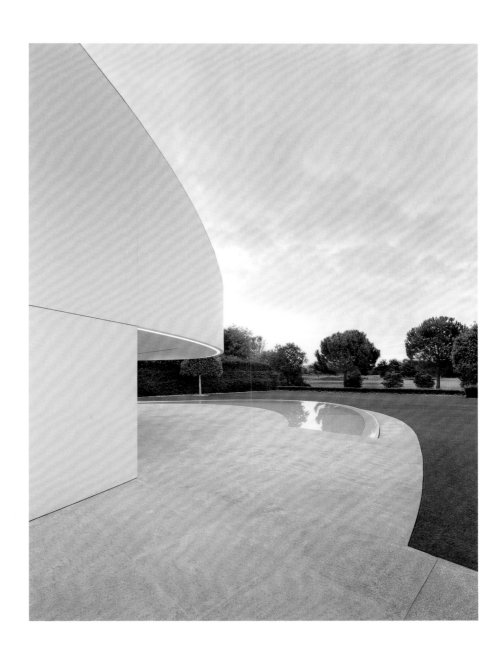

CASSINA. THIS WILL BE THE PLACE

"Just as room typologies
are dissolving,
so too are categories
of furniture."

— ARNO BRANDLHUBER, P. 56

"Space is defined by temporal or temporary provisions ....

And through its furnishings, it can often take on various functions at the same time."

— ARNO BRANDLHUBER, PP. 50–53

CASSINA. THIS WILL BE THE PLACE

CASSINA. THIS WILL BE THE PLACE

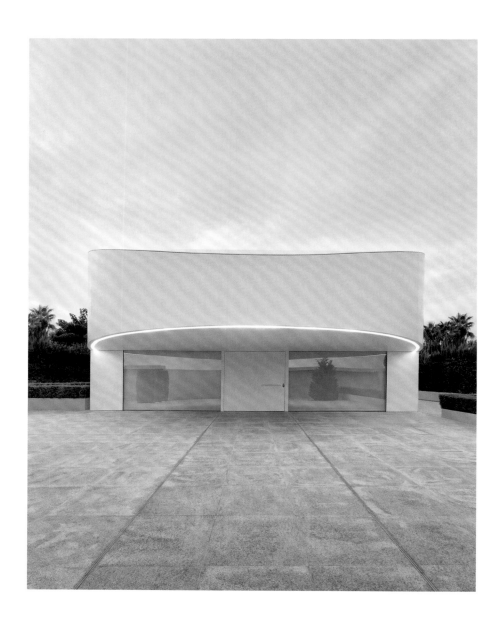

CASSINA. THIS WILL BE THE PLACE

CASSINA. THIS WILL BE THE PLACE

"Space itself has become
a liquid asset ....

thus most new construction
adheres to the principles
of infinite flexibility."

— MARTTI KALLIALA, P. 75

CASSINA. THIS WILL BE THE PLACE

CASSINA. THIS WILL BE THE PLACE

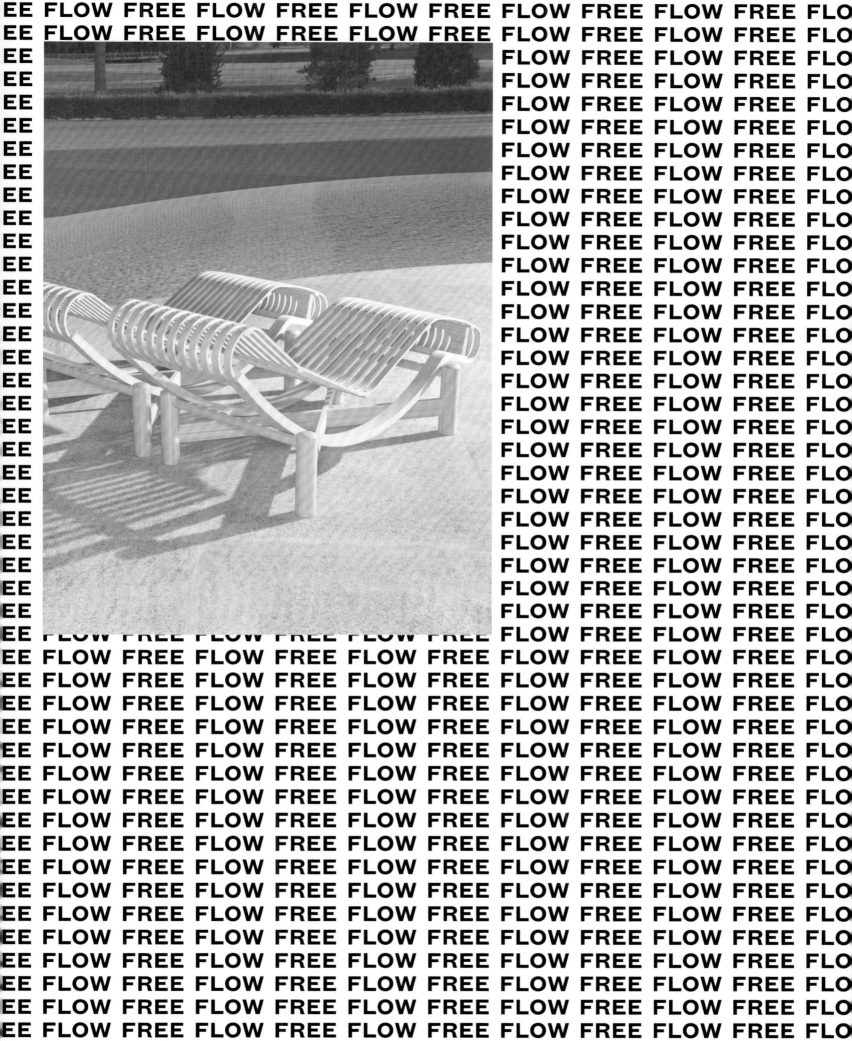

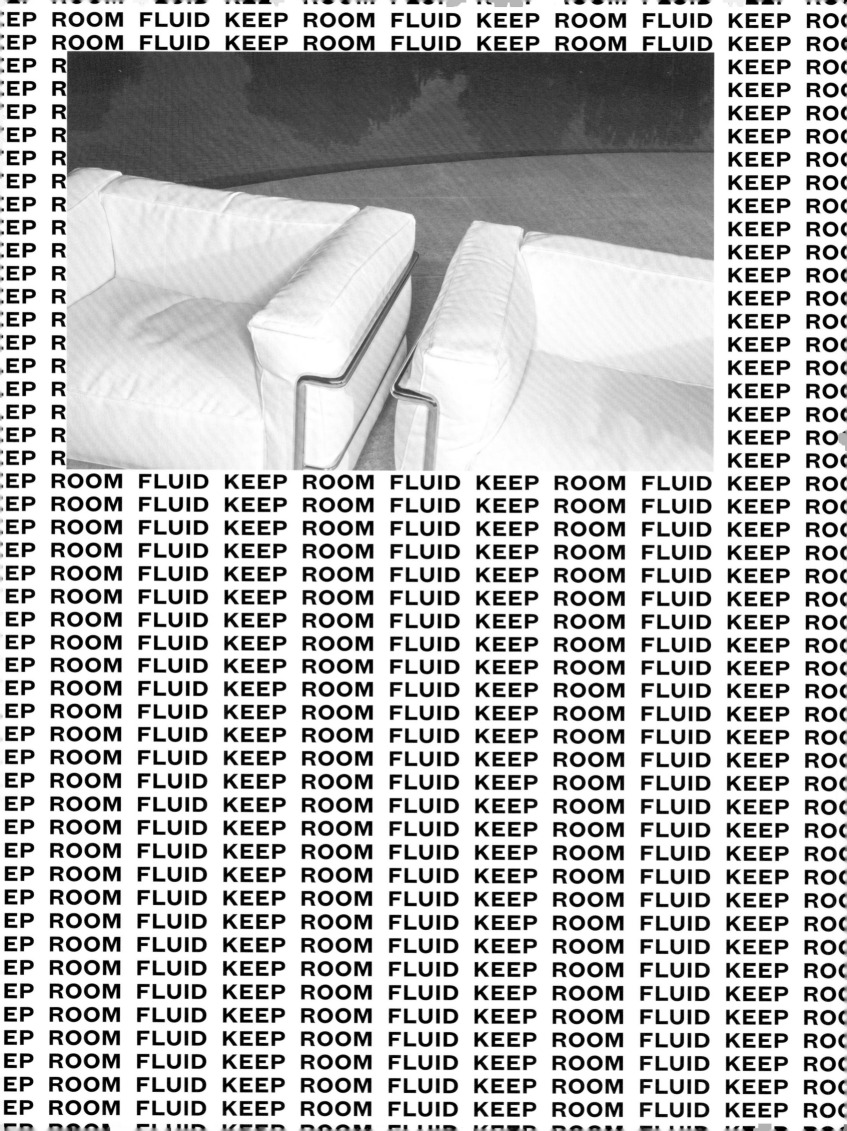

CASSINA. THIS WILL BE THE PLACE

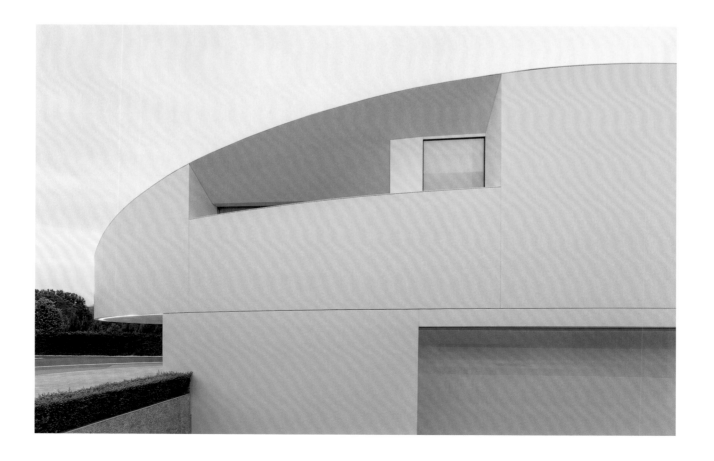

CASSINA. THIS WILL BE THE PLACE

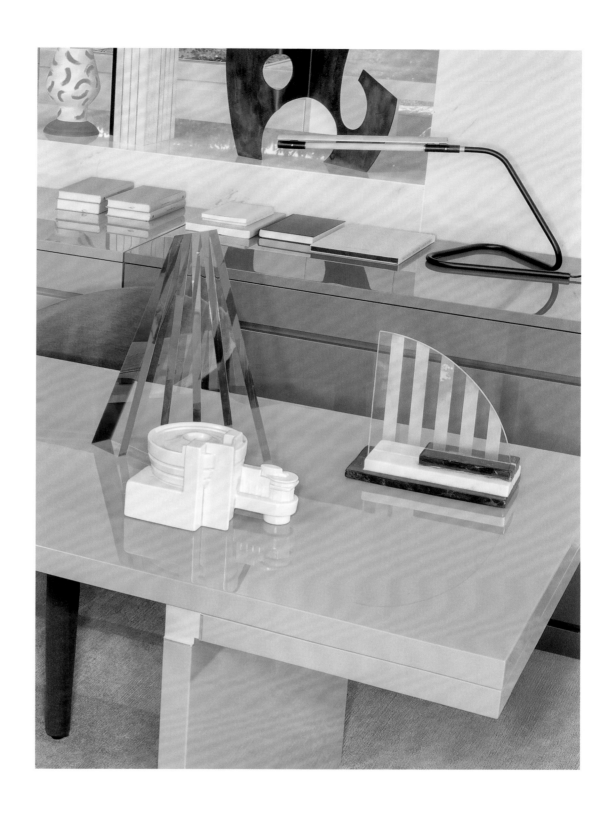

CASSINA. THIS WILL BE THE PLACE

"Just think of the many ways we sit in chairs. There is no one fixed position, but a multitude of different postures.

— KONSTANTIN GRCIC, P. 29

A good chair becomes part of you, it dresses you."

CASSINA. THIS WILL BE THE PLACE

"Furniture is critical
for the house because
it suggests the program
in an open fluid space."

— ZHAO YANG, P. 65

CASSINA. THIS WILL BE THE PLACE

CASSINA. THIS WILL BE THE PLACE

CASSINA. THIS WILL BE THE PLACE

"You don't know if it's a living room or work area.

That has a lot to do with the furniture and the objects that make a room what it is."

— ARNO BRANDLHUBER, P. 50

"You no longer have this separation between public and private.

— ARNO BRANDLHUBER, PP. 54–55

It becomes a kind of open organism."

ARTFUL LIVING

Curated enchantment, a *gesamt* work of art. From the floors
to the ceilings, from the plinths to the frames. A palate
for texture, an orgy of space. An arena of plenty that excels
in restraint. Uniqueness comes twofold, discretion advised.
A symphonic utopia where life imitates art.

CASSINA. THIS WILL BE THE PLACE

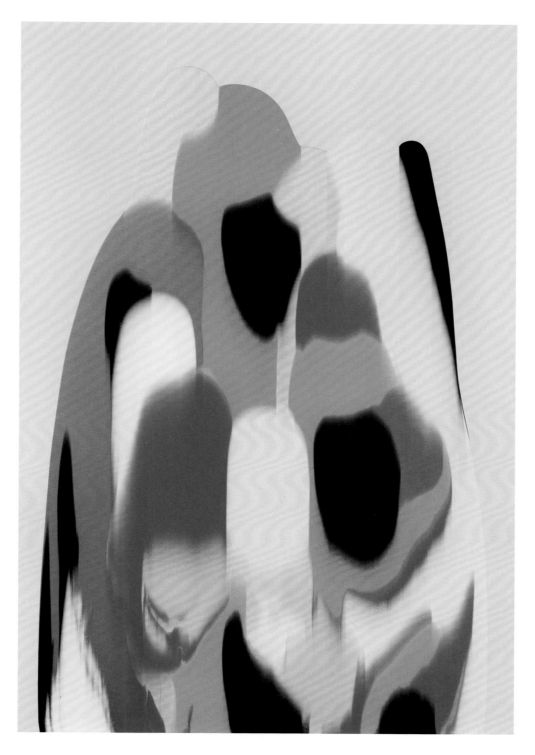

Stefan Behlau, *Blue Footed Booby*, 2015. Acrylic on canvas, 200 x 135 cm (78 ¾ x 53 in)

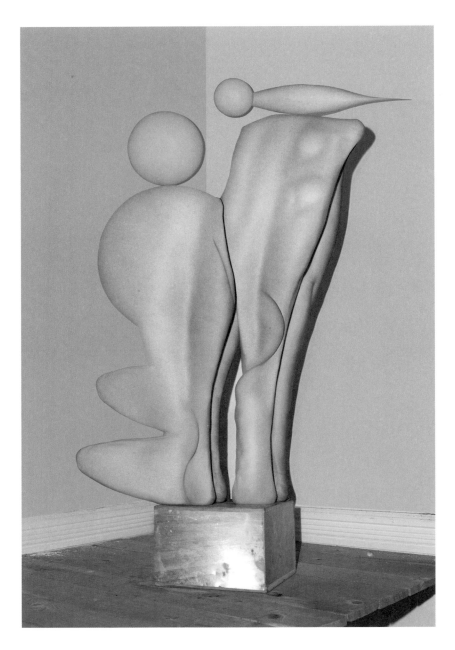

Asger Carlsen, *Spooner Orgie #1*, 2017. Pigment print, 60 x 80 cm (23 ⅝ x 31 ½ in)

Stefan Behlau, *Untitled IV*, 2015. Acrylic on canvas, 200 x 160 cm (78 ¾ x 63 in)

On the chair: Enrico Boccioletti, *Daisy Bunce, χλμ Αθηνών 239, 2332 ΛΑΚΑΤΑΜΕΙΑ*, 2012. 54 x 43 x 4 cm (21 ¼ x 17 x 1 ½ in)

**"If I bought a chair today, for example,
I'd buy thirty right away and put them everywhere.
You can slide them together sometimes,
or arrange them in threes. Or not."**

— Arno Brandlhuber, pp. 55-56

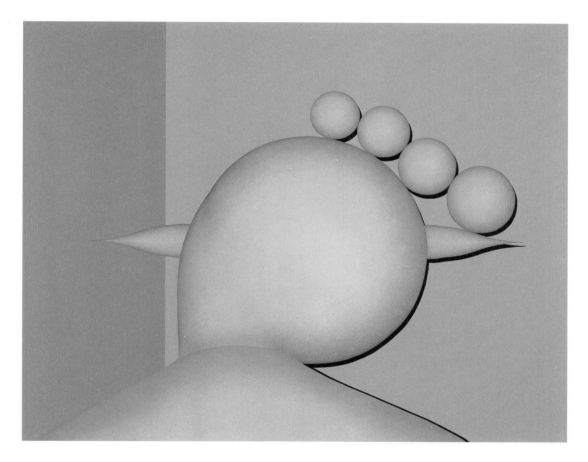

Asger Carlsen, *Spooner Orgie #1*, 2017. Pigment print, 60 x 80 cm (23 ⅝ x 31 ½ in)

Left: Laureline Galliot, *JUG prototype*, 2012. 3-D printing, inkjet powder, 12 x 22.5 x 22 cm (4 ¾ x 8 ⅞ x 8 ¾ in)
Right: Laureline Galliot, *Lucky Toad Vase*, prototype, 2013. 3-D printing, inkjet powder, 20 x 19 x 30 cm (7 ⅞ x 7 ½ x 11 ⅞ in)

"These domestic spaces are occupied by sparse arrangements and assemblages of affective objects, to be reconfigured or completely redone in a cycle of four to twelve weeks. Not primarily to be lived in, or to be used, but to be mediated, contemplated, and consumed as images."

— Martti Kalliala, p. 71

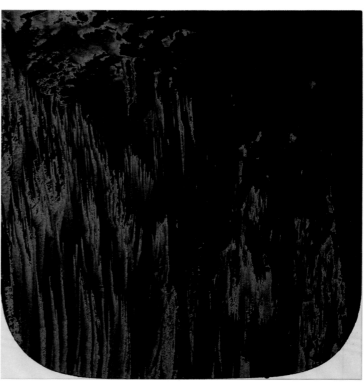

Stefan Behlau, *Cave*, 2011. Acrylic and inkjet on canvas, 97 x 95.5 and 101 x 95.5 cm (38 ¼ x 37 ⅝ and 39 ¾ x 37 ⅝ in)

Stefan Behlau, *Untitled*, 2014. Acrylic on canvas, 200 x 150 cm (78 ¾ x 59 in)

Background wall, left: Asger Carlsen, *Spooner Budy #3*, 2017, pigment print, 60 x 80 cm (23 ⅝ x 31 ½ in)

"Time—and with it culture—is a spiral: everything that once was will return, but in different form. We will live tomorrow as we lived in the past—only differently."

— Martti Kalliala, p. 79

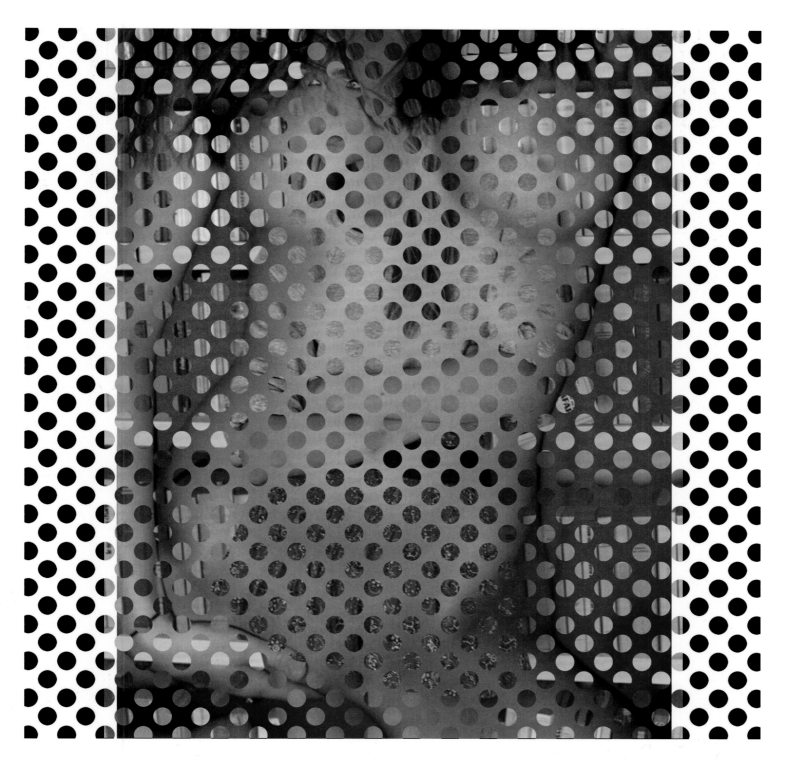

Stefan Behlau, *Keep It Out / Let It In*, 2011. Acrylic, polymer, and inkjet on canvas, 101 x 101 cm (39 ¾ x 39 ¾ in)

CASSINA. THIS WILL BE THE PLACE

Asger Carlsen, *Spooner Budy #2*, 2017. Pigment print, 60 x 80 cm (23 ⅝ x 31 ½ in)

Background wall, right: Asger Carlsen, *Spooner With Cock*, 2017. Pigment print, 60 x 80 cm (23 ⅝ x 31 ½ in)

"As stated by Chogyam Trungpa, 'Art involves relating with oneself and one's phenomenal world gracefully'."

— Zhao Yang, p. 66

CASSINA. THIS WILL BE THE PLACE

"Liberated from a pledge to utility, these spaces surpass the beauty of any abode of today."

— Martti Kalliala, p. 71

CASSINA. THIS WILL BE THE PLACE

Stefan Behlau, *Reverse Untitled 2014*, 2016. Mixed media, 200 x 160 cm (78 ¾ x 63 in)

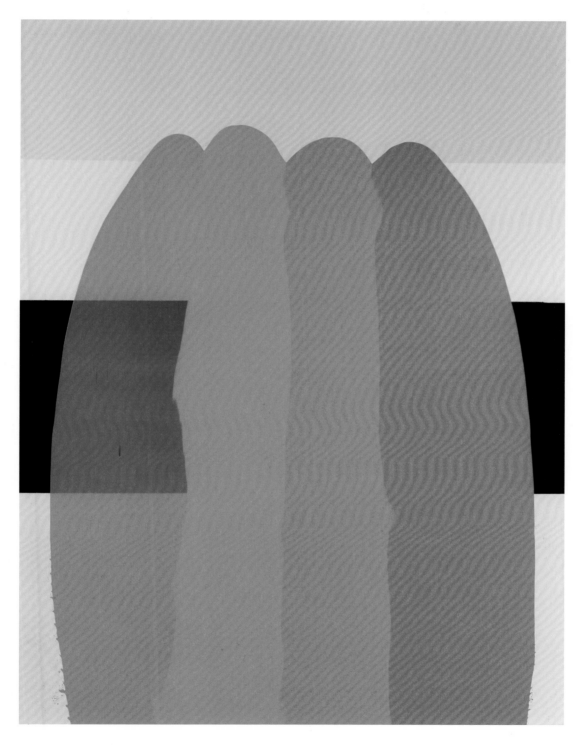

Stefan Behlau, *Orange Cadmium Deep Organic*, 2014. Acrylic and silkscreen ink on canvas, 200 x 150 cm (78 ¾ x 59 ⅛ in)

"Design is not about changing things
for the sake of change. Design should not be imposing,
but rather make an offering, a proposal."

— Konstantin Grcic, p. 32

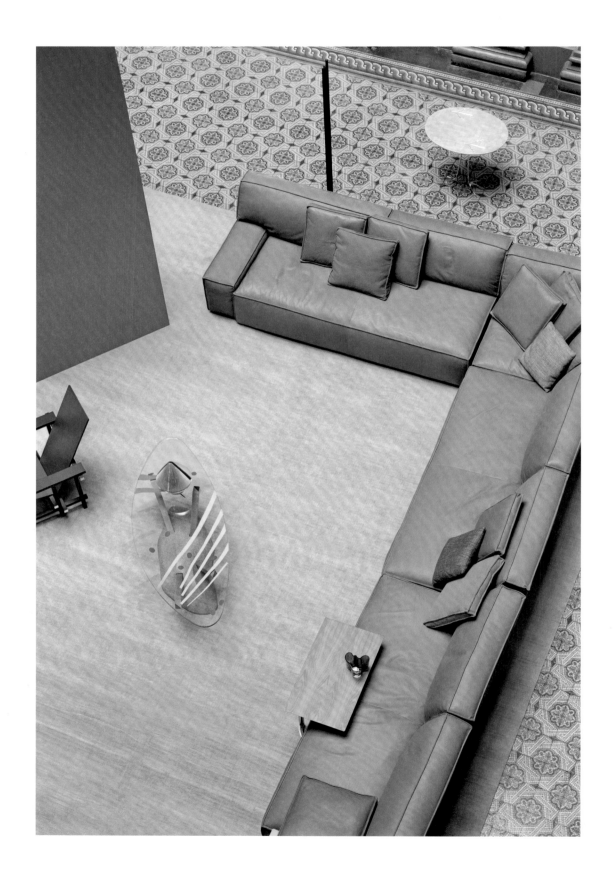

CASSINA. THIS WILL BE THE PLACE

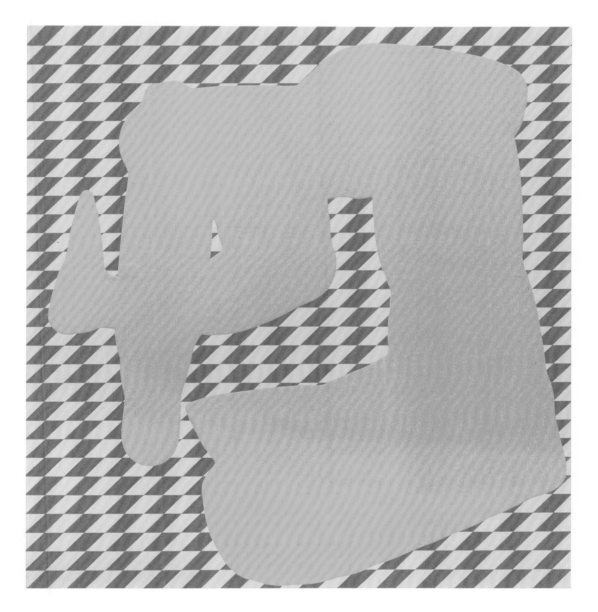

Stefan Behlau, *Ysork*, 2016. Acrylic on canvas, 150 x 140 cm (59 x 55 ⅛ in)

Pink object: Analogia Project, *Booming Vases*, Limited Edition, 2014. Ceramic, porcelain, dimensions vary
Mirror sculpture: Marco Klefisch, *Minotaur*, 2015. Mirror glass and wood, 25 x 25 x 35 cm (9 ⅞ x 9 ⅞ x 13 ⅞ in)

CASSINA. THIS WILL BE THE PLACE

Stefan Behlau, *American Falls*, 2012. Inkjet on canvas, 100 x 200 cm (39 ⅜ x 78 ¾ in)

Stefan Behlau, *Betty White*, 2012. Acrylic and inkjet on canvas, 101 x 71 cm (39 ¾ x 28 in)

Stefan Behlau, *Untitled*, 2014. Acrylic on canvas, 200 cm x 160 cm (78 ¾ x 63 in)

PLAYGROUND

ALERT TO THE THRILL OF A HYBRID EXISTENCE. DELIGHTFUL DISRUPTIONS PLAY GAMES WITH ONE'S MIND. COLOR AND TEXTURE, SURFACE AND DEPTH. TACTILE LIKE SCULPTURE, PERCEPTIVE TO TOUCH. A NEW DOMESTICITY EXERCISES ITS GRIP. NEVER NOT TIMELESS AND ALWAYS AHEAD.

CASSINA. THIS WILL BE THE PLACE

CASSINA. THIS WILL BE THE PLACE

"THE IDEAL OBJECTS OF THE FUTURE SHOULD MAKE SOMETHING POSSIBLE. MAKE SOMETHING EASIER."

— ARNO BRANDLHUBER, P. 56

CASSINA. THIS WILL BE THE PLACE

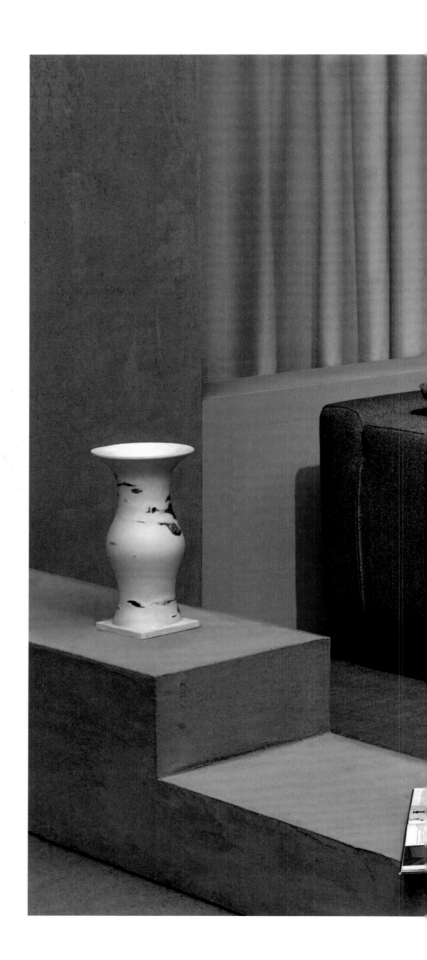

CASSINA. THIS WILL BE THE PLACE

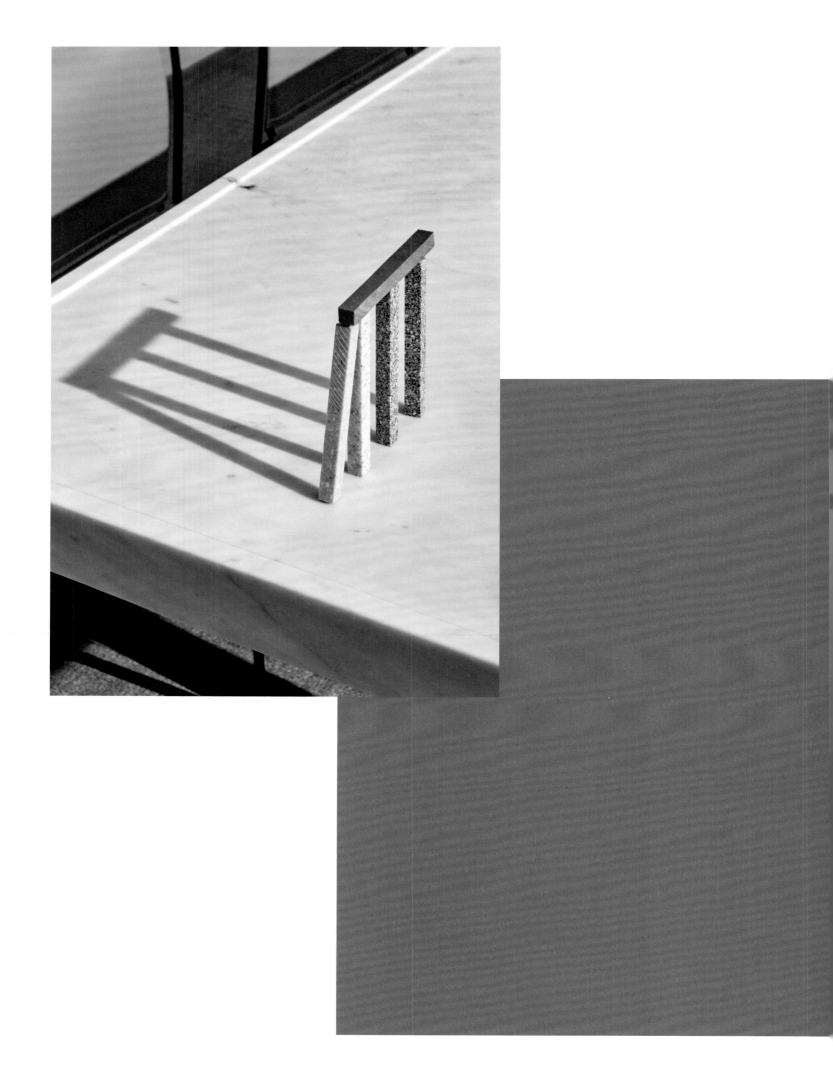

CASSINA. THIS WILL BE THE PLACE

"OBJECTS SHOULDN'T BE SO FIXED, BECAUSE THE SPACES IN WHICH WE LIVE NO LONGER ARE EITHER."

— ARNO BRANDLHUBER, P. 56

CASSINA. THIS WILL BE THE PLACE

"DESIGN IS AN ACT OF EMANCIPATION. WHILE OUR LIFE IS SUBJECT TO CERTAIN CONDITIONS, DESIGN ENABLES US TO CHANGE THESE CONDITIONS."

— KONSTANTIN GRCIC, P. 34

CASSINA. THIS WILL BE THE PLACE

"THESE HOMES HAVE BEEN RETROFITTED WITH UNEVEN FLOORS (TO KEEP ONE ALERT) AND A VARIETY OF VERTICAL AND HORIZONTAL BARS, HANDLES, GRIPS, ROPES, SLINGS, AND RINGS (TO STIMULATE MOVEMENT) THAT HAVE SEEMINGLY REPLACED ANYTHING TRADITIONALLY UNDERSTOOD AS 'FURNISHING.' THE 3-D LANDSCAPE OF THE HOUSE, IN COMBINATION WITH THE BODY'S FRICTION, PRODUCES AN AESTHETICS OF RESISTANCE TO CORPOREAL COMPLACENCY."

— MARTTI KALLIALA, P. 77

CASSINA. THIS WILL BE THE PLACE

CASSINA. THIS WILL BE THE PLACE

CASSINA. THIS WILL BE THE PLACE

CASSINA. THIS WILL BE THE PLACE

CASSINA. THIS WILL BE THE PLACE

"WHAT'S INTERESTING ABOUT OUR TIMES IS THAT WE'RE NOW CLEARLY LIVING IN A NEW KIND OF HYBRID SPACE."

— BEATRIZ COLOMINA, P. 43

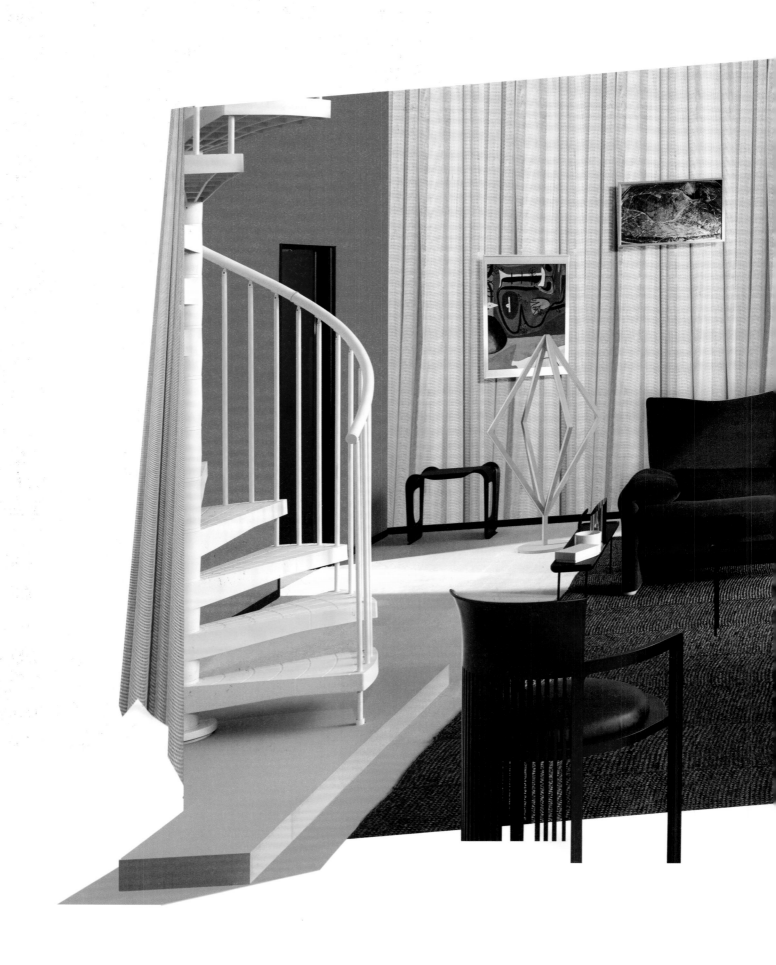

"MOST NEW CONSTRUCTION ADHERES TO THE PRINCIPLES OF INFINITE FLEXIBILITY. A 'HOME' IS ONLY ONE OF THE POSSIBLE PROFIT GENERATING CONCOCTIONS THAT CAN FLOW THROUGH SPACE."

— MARTTI KALLIALA, P. 75

Back To The Roots

A raw taste for nature, a penchant for fresh.
Return to the senses, abound in one's nest.
The view to the past is a vision ahead,
modest in thinking but rich to the touch.
Refinement and beauty with a feeling for less.
An environment of comfort unfinished in bliss.

At the center of the table:
Kazuhito Nagasawa, *The Place Where
Seeds Have Fallen*, 2015, clay, wood
(camphor), aluminum

CASSINA. THIS WILL BE THE PLACE

CASSINA. THIS WILL BE THE PLACE

Keiji Ito, *Tura*, terracotta, Japan

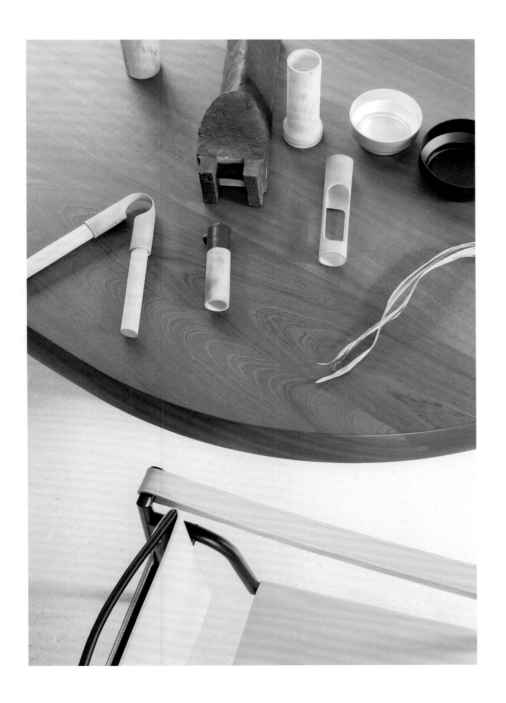

CASSINA. THIS WILL BE THE PLACE

Background, left: Young Ran Lee,
contemporary Japanese pottery

CASSINA. THIS WILL BE THE PLACE

"Driftwood assemblages, dried flowers, and the occasional flotsam of industrial civilization adorn the sensually austere interiors of these arcadian huts, creating the perfect post-information-industrial idyll."

— Martti Kalliala, p. 79

On the bookcase, top:
Shozo Michikawa,
Kohiki Sculptural Form, stoneware

On the bookcase, center:
Shozo Michikawa,
Natural Ash Sculptural Form,
2015, stoneware

Lower left:
Aart Van Asseldonk,
It's healthy to piss out the fire candelabrum,
2015, bronze, Plusdesign Gallery

CASSINA. THIS WILL BE THE PLACE

Objects by French designer Samy Rio: research on bamboo
as a semi-worked product, a natural and sustainable alternative
to industrially produced objects.

"The TERRA SEAT communicates that Man's most natural act since the beginning—that of 'sitting on the ground'—is performed today with a certain awkwardness; we don't know how to do it anymore: beyond the dictates of logic, the earth is now felt to lie below a cold slab, like some unattainable relic."

—Alessandro Mendini

CASSINA. THIS WILL BE THE PLACE

CASSINA. THIS WILL BE THE PLACE

CASSINA. THIS WILL BE THE PLACE

CASSINA. THIS WILL BE THE PLACE

"We enjoy the process of building up
a rich understanding of a place and its
people, then providing something that
looks as if it grew there naturally."

— Zhao Yang, p. 66

In glass case:
Yasuhisa Kohyama, *Suemono*, 2014, stoneware

CASSINA. THIS WILL BE THE PLACE

CASSINA. THIS WILL BE THE PLACE

"When there's an existing structure, it always has value—regardless of whether it's a beautiful old design object or a horrible relic from the dump."

—Arno Brandlhuber, p. 51

CASSINA. THIS WILL BE THE PLACE

"Luckily the root of this culture is just too stubborn to be destroyed. It's very profound, and still exists in the subconscious of most people brought up in this culture."

— Zhao Yang, p. 61

CASSINA. THIS WILL BE THE PLACE

Keiji Ito, *Two Turas*, 2014, terracotta

CASSINA. THIS WILL BE THE PLACE

"The typology of the chair has been around since ancient Egypt, if not longer. But for all its simplicity, it has always had an enormous capacity to adapt or even anticipate the changes in society."

— Konstantin Grcic, p. 28

CASSINA. THIS WILL BE THE PLACE

CASSINA. THIS WILL BE THE PLACE

The creation of life from the confines of the lounge. Connected from flatness into a space of its own. One plane, three dimensions, all day and all night. Between cotton and data lies a braver new world. Profound in its impact, yet so soft at its core.

In the age of global connectedness
we are actors and authors at the same time.
We share images and words,
from any place, at any given time.

The bed is not just an instrument
designed for relaxation—it's a place
where things are produced, invented, planned.
A fluid and dynamic dimension, like a film set,
where we become the protagonists
and interpreters of contemporary life.

I WOULD TRAVEL ANYWHERE IN THE WORLD ON MY BED.

AND YET THE OUTSIDE WORLD CAN WAIT, BECAUSE DIGITAL IMAGES REPLACE NATURAL SCENARIOS.
THERE'S NO NEED TO GO ANYWHERE. EVERYTHING YOU NEED IS WITHIN REACH.

THE BED IS AT THE CENTER OF THE HOUSE... WHERE NEW STORIES CAN BE DRAFTED,
AND THOSE OF OTHERS CAN BE DISCUSSED.

REAL PERCEPTION AND HI-TECH IMAGINATION.
BOTH OF THESE ELEMENTS THRIVE IN THE SAME ENVIRONMENT.
THE BORDERS BETWEEN HOME AND OFFICE DISSOLVE.

*THE BED IS THE ONLY PLACE WHERE YOU CAN READ
AND THE BEST PLACE TO TALK ON THE PHONE.*

CREATIVITY HAS TWO ESSENTIAL STAGES:
THE BED AND THE WORLD.

IDEAS, REFLECTIONS, AND INSIGHTS
ARE SURROUNDED BY EVERYDAY OBJECTS.

EVERY SINGLE INSTANT WE PRODUCE DATA, INFORMATION,
AND PHOTOS ACCESSIBLE TO ALL.

BEDTIME IS DAYTIME!

CASSINA. THIS WILL BE THE PLACE

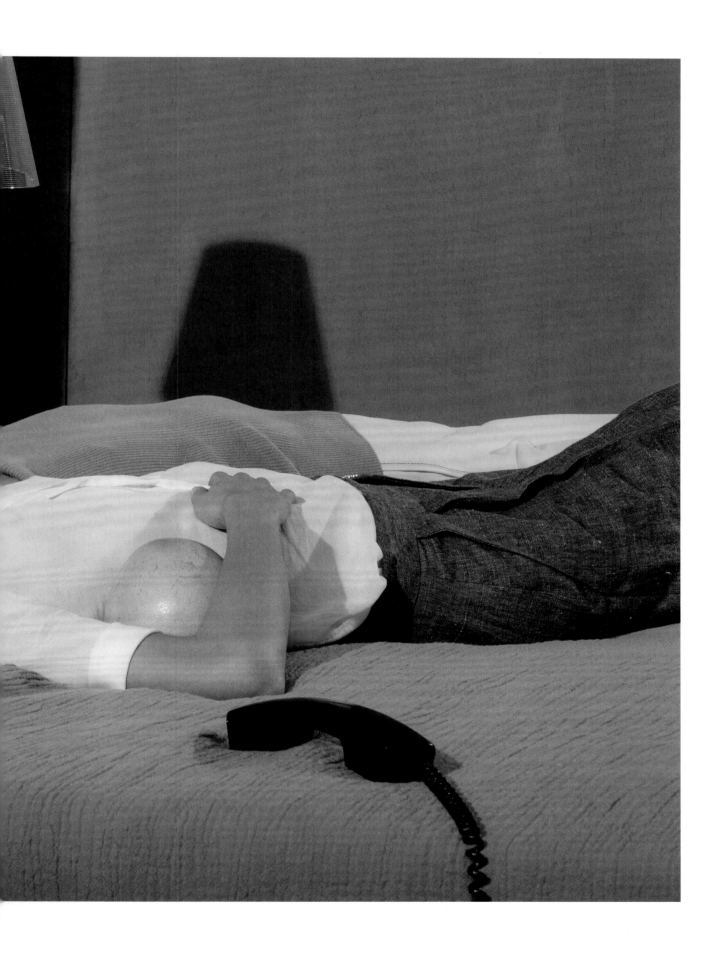

A CONSIDERATION FOR SPACE DOWN TO THE MOST MINUTE DETAIL.

TO CREATE THE PERFECT SETTING.
THE IMPECCABLE BACKDROP FOR THE PHOTO STILLS OF ONE'S LIFE.

BARRIERS FALL. WALLS VANISH. WE SLEEP WHERE WE INVENT.
WE EAT WHERE WE PRODUCE. WE THINK WHERE WE ACT.

CASSINA. THIS WILL BE THE PLACE

WE MOVE THROUGH SPACE, FINDING OUR NOTES
AND OUR POST-ITS EVERYWHERE, LIKE AN AUTHOR'S ANNOTATIONS
READY FOR PUBLICATION.

THE INTERNET IS NOT ANOTHER WORLD.
IT IS THE MOST POWERFUL TOOL IN THE WORLD.

WHO NEEDS A DESK TO WORK?

MOVE IN HERE. IT'S WONDERFUL.
THE SUN ALWAYS SHINES.

YOU THINK BETTER WHEN YOU'RE FACING UPWARD.

CASSINA. THIS WILL BE THE PLACE

TIME EXPANDS. DOES THE DAY TURN INTO EVENING
OR DOES EVENING MERGE INTO THE DAY?

I DON'T CARE WHAT TIME IT IS.
I'M ALWAYS CONNECTED.

PRIVACY-NON-PRIVACY. IN THE AGE OF CONSTANT EXPOSURE
THERE IS NO APPARENT SOLITUDE.

REGARDLESS OF SECRET EMOTIONS.

CASSINA. THIS WILL BE THE PLACE

REGARDLESS OF SMALL DISTRACTIONS.

IN THIS NEW WAY OF INHABITING SPACE, DIGITAL COEXISTS
SIDE BY SIDE WITH REALITY, THE FORMAL WITH THE INFORMAL,
WORK WITH PLAY, CALM WITH ACTION.

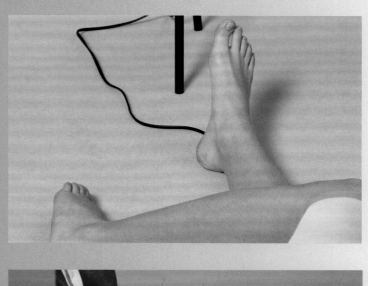

THERE IS NO BOUNDARY BETWEEN PUBLIC AND PRIVATE ANYMORE.
HOW MANY PEOPLE CAN SEE OUR BEDROOM?

HOW MANY PEOPLE CAN LIKE THE FURNITURE WE CHOOSE?
HOW MANY PEOPLE KNOW WHAT TIME WE WAKE UP?

HOW MANY PEOPLE DO WE LET INTO OUR HOME?

LIFE BECOMES EASIER WHEN YOU HAVE THE PERFECT BED.

The bed is like a bridge
suspended over the world.
With no limits or schedules.
No rules or limits.

Bigger and bigger,
more and more comfortable,
more and more efficient,
more and more important.

Reference Chart

FREE FLOW

Photography   Beppe Brancato
Location   Balint House, Bétera, Valencia, Spain
Architecture   Fran Silvestre Arquitectos

Armstoel van gebogen triplex
Gerrit Thomas Rietveld, ca. 1930
Study model, 1974
Cassina Historical Archives
| pp. 84/86/89 |

Sindbad
Vico Magistretti, Cassina 1981
Cassina Historical Archives
| pp. 122/123 |

ARTFUL LIVING

Photography Beppe Brancato
Location Villa Erba, Cernobbio, Como, Italy
Architecture Angelo Savoldi,
Giovan Battista Borsani

Heritage Henredon chair
Frank Lloyd Wright, 1955
Study model, 1992
Cassina Historical Archives
| pp. 151/152 |

Midway 1
Frank Lloyd Wright, 1914
Cassina, 1986
Cassina Historical Archives
| p. 156 |

Berlijnse stoel
Gerrit Thomas Rietveld, 1923
Study model, 1974
Cassina Historical Archives
| pp. 162/165 |

Sansonedue
Gaetano Pesce, Cassina 1987
Cassina Historical Archives
| pp. 138/168/170/172 |

Chair for Waitress
Charles Rennie Mackintosh, 1904
Study model, 1971
Cassina Historical Archives
| p. 172 |

Artifici
Paolo Deganello, Cassina 1985
Cassina Historical Archives
| pp. 177/178 |

Krukje-Tafeltje
Gerrit Thomas Rietveld, 1923
Study model, 1974
Cassina Historical Archives
| p. 177 |

PLAYGROUND

Photography Leonardo Scotti
Collage Fausto Fantinuoli
Location Studio Fotografico Sardi
Cernusco sul Naviglio, Milan, Italy

Taliesin West
Frank Lloyd Wright, 1949
Cassina, 1986
Cassina Historical Archives
| p. 193 |

Nitshill High
Charles Rennie Mackintosh, 1903
Cassina 1989
Cassina Historical Archives
| p. 196 |

Tangram
Massimo Morozzi, Cassina 1983
Cassina Historical Archives
| pp. 190/201 |

Johnson Wax 2
Frank Lloyd Wright, 1936
Cassina 1991
Cassina Historical Archives
| pp. 203/213 |

Beugelstoel
Gerrit Thomas Rietveld, 1927
Study model, 1974
Cassina Historical Archives
| p. 220 |

BACK TO THE ROOTS

Photography   Beppe Brancato
Location   La Vecchia Finanza
Scopello, Castellammare del Golfo, Italy
Architecture   Brandlhuber + Michalski&Wagner

Steltman stoel
Gerrit Thomas Rietveld, 1963
Study model, 1974
Cassina Historical Archives
| pp. 243/244/245 |

Taliesin 3
Frank Lloyd Wright, 1937
Cassina 1993
Cassina Historical Archives
| pp. 255/257 |

Heritage Henredon Stools
Frank Lloyd Wright, 1955
Study model, 1986
Cassina Historical Archives
| p. 260 |

Terra
Alessandro Mendini
for Bracciodiferro Cassina 1974
Cassina Historical Archives
| p. 263 |

BED TIME

Photography Charles Negre
Copy Giorgia Virzì
Location Studio Fotografico Sardi
Cernusco sul Naviglio, Milan, Italy

Midway 2
Frank Lloyd Wright, 1914
Cassina 1986
Cassina Historical Archives
| p. 306 |

*Chair painted white
and upholstered in linen,
Turin Exhibition*, 1902
Charles Rennie Mackintosh,
Study model, 1973
Cassina Historical Archives
| p. 328 |

Bellini's Perspective

On August 24, 79 AD, at around 1 p.m., Mount Vesuvius exploded unexpectedly. The eruption overwhelmed all the inhabitants of Pompeii, Herculaneum, and the surrounding areas. It buried their homes, their decorations and splendid frescoes, their furnishings, the carpets, mosaics, statues, fountains, kitchens, ovens, sinks, cutlery, pottery, triclinia, curtains, clothes, impluvia, doors, stairs, windows, roofs, gutters, beds, chairs, pillows, portals, cupboards, silverware, footwear, bathrooms, latrines, lamps, scrolls, jewelry, mirrors, working animals as well as pets.

It buried streets, porticoes, shops, squares, markets, roofs, the churches and public buildings of Pompeii and Herculaneum.

It buried everything for 1,700 years, until the excavation campaigns—begun by the Bourbons in the mid-eighteenth century—gradually unearthed an astonishing vision of civilization that was still practically intact. Now it is considered a museum experience unlike any other in the world, and rightly so.

Today, we have no idea whether the people of ancient Rome enjoyed contemplating or predicting the future of humanity, and especially "future lifestyles."

But one thing is for sure: the long roster of objects that were buried does not contain a single term or circumstance that isn't already still familiar to us in the area of so-called Western culture. And this immediately puts everything in a new perspective, because, leaving aside less substantial matters, this would be like saying something that is unquestionably true for me—that almost 2,000 years later all of us today still "live" the same way.

And if Pompeiians had ever asked themselves questions about their future, no doubt such questions would never have been about the "Home of the Future." Such questions did not become popular until the nineteenth century, thanks to Jules Verne first, and increasingly continued to be tackled as a host of new materials, innovative procedures for making things, and increasingly efficient and automatic climatization methods became available.

These thoughts are meant to broach the two extremes of the issue: on the one hand, confidence in the future and in the continuous innovations available, which stimulate the tendency to envision other-directed scenarios for the home, and view the inhabitant as an enterprising experimenter, almost an extra in a science fiction or architecture fiction movie. On the other hand, a school of thought that sees science, technology, and materials as a means for always getting the best performance at the lowest cost, while maintaining at the core, however, the role of the human being as the custodian of a deeply rooted culture of habitation.

A culture of habitation that is inherent to one's native geographical or historical area, and to one's traditions: urban, rural, metropolitan, nomadic, religious, commercial, financial, artisanal. And all with the relative tendencies toward stationariness and continuity, toward mobility and the influence of one's job or profession and role, even when this means radical geographical resettlement.

But do we really need to ask ourselves questions in order to shed light on the "Home of the Future"?

Lawrence Alma-Tadema, *Interior of Gaius Marcius's House*, Manchester Art Gallery

The "Home of the Future" or the "Future of the Home" is *us*. We are the actors and protagonists of the present time, which we inhabit in every corner of the world, heirs to our past, but forward-looking too, speaking all our languages, plus one lingua franca: the language of chairs and tables, beds and sofas, the language of chandeliers and *abat-jours*, of pillows and carpets, the language of chaise longues and armchairs, the language of walls and doors, windows, floors, and ceilings.

It is a language built up by generation after generation, one that is constantly evolving amidst inventions, variations, and refrains, a living language that we never stop learning and that we never grow weary of speaking. A language that we all use and that ultimately represents us by talking about us and for us. It is the noble language of everyday living.

It was within this context that in the mid-1970s, having felt the need to give a more systematic and incisive perspective to the many furnishings I was designing for Cassina, I decided to collect and document them in two volumes, ironically (but not too much so) called *Il libro dell'arredamento secondo Mario Bellini* (The Book of Interior Decor by Mario Bellini); one of them was devoted to "tables" (something that has always been my passion), and the other to "upholstered furniture."

I gave my tables names from architecture: "Il Castello/The Castle," "La Rotonda/The Rotunda," "Il Colonnato/The Colonnade," "La Corte/The Court," "La Basilica/The Basilica"… because tables are truly microarchitectures. Not

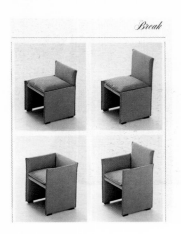
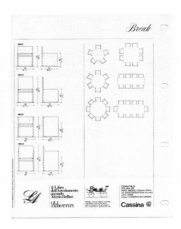

From *Il libro dell'arredamento secondo Mario Bellini* published by the Centro Cesare Cassina in two volumes in 1976 and 1977

Two portraits, taken exactly fifty years apart, of Mario Bellini sitting in the 932, an armchair produced in 1967 and now aesthetically and technically updated

Antonello da Messina, *Saint Jerome in His Study*, London, National Gallery

Tutankhamun's chair-throne, Cairo, Egyptian Museum

CASSINA. THIS WILL BE THE PLACE

simply a raised platform but so much more. It is no accident that people play, sign peace and war treaties, eat three meals a day as well as the Last Supper on tables…

I instead chose the names of carriages for my chairs: "Break," "Whiskey," "Tilbury," "Clarence," and "Duc." And then "Char-à-Banc," "Fiacre," "Landeau," and "Coupé" for the beds. Was this just some game? Yes, but I was also being serious. Because it tended to connect the elite world of "design" to real life and its (and our) solid historical roots. These books (which I am hoping will be reprinted) have become collectors' items, but those names—and those things —have steadfastly endured to challenge time.

Mario Bellini

PS: To make sure you're still pondering over this, here are four questions still awaiting an answer:
1—Why do buildings and interior decor last so long over time while machines in general instantly become obsolete?
2—Why does so much of what concerns the inhabitable sphere stubbornly resist industrialization, that is to say, the mass production of a few tried and tested models according to prevalently "functional" criteria?
3—Can Antonello da Messina's *Saint Jerome in His Study* be used as a key to better understand today's home and office?
4—Who designed Tutankhamun's throne-cum-chair? Where does its structural architecture come from, and why is it still so reminiscent of a chair of our own?

Credits

The text published on pages 290-335 are by Giorgia Virzì.

All the pictures are from the Cassina Archives except the following:

© Achim Hatzius, pp. 51, 54
© Adoc Photos / Contrasto, p. 23, centre
© Akg Images / Contrasto, p. 42
© Archives Charlotte Perriand, p. 13, above
© Archivio Scala, Firenze, p. 346, right
© Bettmann / Getty Images, p. 41
© CCA Centre Canadien d'Architecture, Montréal, p. 36
© Christopher Rau, p. 48
© Efrem Raimondi, p. 10, above
© Entertainment Pictures / Eyevine / Contrasto, p. 24
© Erica Overmeer, p. 121, right
© Fien Muller, p. 52
© Fondation Le Corbusier, pp. 32, 33, 40, 55, 66, 347
© Fondazione Franco Albini, p. 11, above
© Foto Matteo Imbriani, p. 12
© Foto Ranzini (Valerio Castelli), p. 18
© Gabriele Basilico, p. 10, below
© Giulio Calderini, pp. 4-5
© Hans Hollein, p. 46
© Hao Chen Hchen, p. 63
© Jean Baptiste Mondino, p. 14, above
© John Kobal Foundation / Getty Images, p. 25, below
© Jonathan Leijonhufvud, pp. 58, 64, 65, 121, right
© Konstantin Grcic Industrial Design, p. 29
© Konstantin Grcic Industrial Design and Galerie Max
        Hetzler, Berlin-Paris / def image, p. 31
© Manchester Art Gallery, UK / Bridgeman Images, p. 343
© Markus Jans, p. 26
© Matthew Donaldson, p. 14, above
© Mondadori Portfolio, p. 25, above
© Nathan Willock pp. 50, 56
© National Gallery, London, UK / Bridgeman Images,
        p. 346, left
© Paavo Lehtonen, p. 68
© Paris Match / photo by Walter Carone / Getty Images,
        p. 39
© Pengfei Wang, p. 60
© Peter Kainz / MAK, p. 53
© Rietveld Schröder Archief / Centraal Museum Utrecht /
        Pictoright, p. 6
© Rue des Archives / Mondadori Portfolio, p. 23, above
© Salvatore Gozzo, p. 121, left
© Shawn Maximo, p. 30
© Simon Watson, p. 52
© Warner Bros Pictures / Mondadori Portfolio,
        p. 23, below

Artists
Asger Carlsen, Courtesy Dittrich & Schlechtriem, Berlin
Enrico Boccioletti
Stefan Behlau, Courtesy Dittrich & Schlechtriem,
        Berlin – Photos © Jens Ziehe
Laureline Galliot, *Lucky toad & cat ipad painting*,
        2014, p. 235
Mathieu Peyroulet Ghilini, *Flowerpot*, 2016, pp. 193, 194,
        199; *Holidays #003*, 2016, p. 227; *Holidays #009*,
        p. 236

Thanks to
Mario Bellini
Beppe Brancato
Stefano De Monte
Charles Negre
Nicola Zocchi

The Publisher remains at the disposal of claimants
for any sources not identified.

Aknowledgments

Thanks to Patricia Urquiola, Art Director Cassina.

Thanks for their kind help to:
Andrew Ayers
Elena Marco
Frank Mecking
Martin Estrade
Jenna Krumminga

Casting Director: Irene Barra
Fashion Styling: Francesca Izzi
Hair-Makeup: Luciano Chiarello
Irene Arescaldino
Dimitra Marlanti

Aart Van Asseldonk
Alessi
Analogia Project
Anglepoise
Artemide
Atipico
Bang & Olufsen
Bitossi Ceramiche
Bolon
Brionvega
Budri
Calcaterra
Carlo Moretti
Catellani&Smith
Chiara Andreatti
Danese Milano
Dedar
Dondup
Eligo
Ermenegildo Zegna
Federica Elmo
Flos
Fontanot
Glas Italia
Golran
Iittala
Kazuhito Nagasawa
Kinnasand
Lalique
Lanificio Colombo
Lardini
Listone Giordano
Liuni
Lualdi
Luceplan
Lucio Vanotti
Marco Klefisch
Mingardo Designer Faber
Moreschi
Nemo Lighting
Normann Copenhagen
Officine Saffi
Oikos
Oluce

Paola C
Passaggio S.a.s.
Paul Smith
Penta Light
Piazza Sempione
PlayStation Sony
Plusdesign Gallery
Plus Minus Zero
Pretziada
Samsung
Samy Rio
Shozo Michikawa
Smeg
Society Limonta
Sowden
Stefano Russo For Siens Eye Code
Studio Testo
Sunnei
Vano Alto
VCS
Venini
Wallpepper
Yasuhisa Kohyama
Young Ran Lee

This Will Be The Place

Edited by
Felix Burrichter

Concept and Art Direction
Cassina

Book Design
Giulia Dolci

Contributors
Barbara Lehmann
          Head of Cassina Historical Archives
Mario Bellini
Arno Brandlhuber
Felix Burrichter
Beatriz Colomina
Konstantin Grcic
Martti Kalliala
Zhao Yang

Art Direction Consulting for Part II
Valentina Cameranesi Sgroi & Enrico Pompili

Translations
Sylvia Adrian Notini

Editorial Coordination
Laura De Tomasi

Editing
Susan Ann White for *Scriptum*, Rome

Cover
© Martti Kalliala

Pages 4-5
© Giulio Calderini

First published in the United States of America in 2017
by Rizzoli International Publications, Inc.
300 Park Avenue South
New York, NY 10010
www.rizzoliusa.com

Originally published in Italian in 2017
by Libri Illustrati Rizzoli
© 2017 Mondadori Electa S.p.A., Milano

2017 2018 2019 2020 / 10 9 8 7 6 5 4 3 2 1
ISBN: 978-0-8478-6074-6
Library of Congress Control Number: 2017935106

Printed in Italy

Printed in March 2017 by NAVA Press S.r.l. (Milan)